28 days
of CLEAN
eating

The Healthy Way
to KICK DIETING
FOREVER

28 days of CLEAN eating

The Healthy Way
to KICK DIETING
FOREVER

FALL RIVER PRESS

New York

FALL RIVER PRESS

New York

An Imprint of Sterling Publishing
1166 Avenue of the Americas
New York, NY 10036

FALL RIVER PRESS and the distinctive Fall River Press logo are registered
trademarks of Barnes & Noble, Inc.

© 2014 by Sonoma Press

This publication is intended for informational purposes only. The publisher does
not claim that this publication shall provide or guarantee any benefits, healing,
cure, or any results in any respect. This publication is not intended to provide or
replace conventional medical advice, treatment, or diagnosis or be a substitute to
consulting with a physician or other licensed medical or health-care provider. The
publisher shall not be liable or responsible in any respect for any use or application
of any content contained in this publication or any adverse effects, consequence,
loss, or damage of any type resulting or arising from, directly or indirectly, the
use or application of any content contained in this publication. Any trademarks
are the property of their respective owners, are used for editorial purposes only,
and the publisher makes no claim of ownership and shall acquire no right, title, or
interest in such trademarks by virtue of this publication.

Cover design by Laura Palese

ISBN 978-1-4351-6175-7

For information about custom editions, special sales, and premium and
corporate purchases, please contact Sterling Special Sales at 800-805-5489 or
specialsales@sterlingpublishing.com.

Manufactured in China

2 4 6 8 10 9 7 5 3 1

www.sterlingpublishing.com

Contents

Part II
Eating Clean 73

6

Lunch

7

Snacks

8
Vegetarian Dinners

9
Fish and Seafood Dinners 187

10
Meat and Poultry Dinners 217

11

Dessert   263

12

Kitchen Staples

Introduction
Eating Clean Every Day

Everyone seems to be on some kind of diet or detox these days. It's easy to understand why. Most of us want to live healthier lives, lose a little bit (or a lot) of weight, and generally feel better about the food we put into our bodies. But given what we plan to get out of diets and detoxes, why do they feel more akin to punishment than reward?

For the most part, changing how and what we eat, whether it's for 10 days or 3 months or more, involves restrictions. And math. Certain foods must be cut out. Calories must be counted. Specific foods, regardless of how they taste, must be consumed. Diet fatigue and diet failure happen for a reason. The work involved to diet successfully is exhausting and, due to that very difficulty, it's a struggle to keep it up for the long term. We take a break, and start again later, take another break, start again later, and so on.

Eating healthily does not have to be so hard. It does not need to involve worksheets or calculators. People who have adopted the clean eating "diet" are living these truths firsthand. Clean eating is not a diet in the conventional sense of the word, where you give up certain foods for a period of time to achieve a specific health goal. Clean eating is more of a food philosophy, grounded in the notion that meals should contain all sorts of foods—fruits, vegetables, meats, grains, beans, nuts, and so on. The only restriction is that these foods should be as close as possible to their natural, unadulterated state. Foods should be made of, well, food, rather than combinations of food and chemicals.

Natural does not mean raw. Flip through the recipes in this book and you'll see that clean eating meals make use of an array of ingredients from a variety of cuisines that can be cooked easily and in numerous ways. The 150 recipes offered here are downright delicious and filling, too. From Roasted Butternut Squash and Israeli Couscous Pilaf to Cajun Pork Chops with Grilled Okra and Creamed Corn, you're about to find out that clean eating isn't about restricting what you eat, but expanding your palate with the very best whole, fresh ingredients.

What you will eliminate are processed ingredients. It's true that processed foods tend to be cheap and quick to prepare. It's also true that they are usually high in sodium, refined sugars, additives, preservatives, and unhealthy fats. These ingredients sabotage good health. A clean eating approach to food removes these offenders, and replaces them with "good" fats, whole grains, and protein that will keep you satisfied throughout the day. Eating clean ensures that what you put in your body promotes good health.

In the pages that follow, you'll learn more about how to make clean eating an effortless part of your everyday routine. The four-week meal plan will let you dip your toe in without having to wonder what is and isn't clean. You can shop for the weekly meal plans at your local markets—access to specialty health food stores is not required. What is required is the willingness to give up dieting and allow yourself to enjoy eating. Are you ready?

I

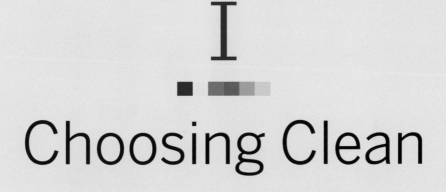

Choosing Clean

1

Cleaning Up
Your Diet

If you've ever bought a prepared spinach dip at the store, odds are that it contained added preservatives, chemicals, and sugar, and more sodium than you wanted or needed. It probably tasted pretty good, too, but those additions aren't necessary to make a flavorful spinach dip—in fact, a homemade version would surely taste even better. The basic ingredients are naturally clean: fresh spinach, full-fat cream cheese, fresh lemon juice, garlic, and freshly ground pepper. Let your taste buds convince you. There's a recipe for Creamy Spinach-Artichoke Dip on page 147.

It's not very difficult to understand what clean eating is in principle, but clean eating in practice can seem challenging at first. This book will get you started and successfully on your way.

Five Principles of Clean Eating

Before embarking on a clean eating plan, it's important to know a bit more about the principles that are at the heart of this lifestyle. The purpose of eating clean is to fuel your body with the healthiest, most natural foods possible. Keep these five important principles in mind:

1 **Choose whole, natural foods and avoid those that are processed and refined.** The easiest way to stick to a clean eating plan is to buy whole foods and cook them yourself, like people did a couple of generations ago, before convenience items were available. When you can, buy local produce, meats, and dairy, which ensures freshness, supports local communities, and is good for the environment, too. Today, more supermarkets than ever before are carrying locally grown and produced items. They are the optimal choices for eating clean. Your best bet is to stay away from packaged food that's traveled from a factory or another country, and processed foods with long ingredient lists.

2 **Read the labels.** When reading packaged food labels, don't let low-fat, no-fat, or reduced-fat fool you. To replace the fat and sugars, unrecognizable compounds have been added to make the product taste better. And who wants to eat something that sounds like a science experiment? A good rule of thumb to go by is: If the label includes more than five ingredients, it's probably not clean. And if an ingredient is unrecognizable or something that does not sit on the shelf in your clean eating pantry (see page 50 for the first of four weekly clean eating pantry lists), it's probably not clean either.

3 **Include some protein, carbohydrate, and fat at every meal.** Eating a balanced diet is the key to staying satisfied throughout the day. The trickiest part for most people is getting enough protein. Protein is crucial for building muscles and it helps you feel energetic longer. Adding a cup of beans to your meal or munching on a handful of nuts is a great way to add protein to your diet. Pay attention to the composition of your meals and be sure they are balanced.

An Inside Look

Processed Food

Foods that come in a box, can, or bag may seem convenient but in reality these products often contain unhealthy ingredients— preservatives and chemicals to lengthen shelf life, and added sugars and fats to enhance flavor.

One ingredient that's often added to processed food is phosphates. As reported in online health magazine *Rodale News*, higher-than-normal phosphate levels in adults have been linked to health problems such as kidney deterioration and weakened bones. Another sneaky ingredient lurking in processed foods is sugar. Whether in the form of refined sugar or high-fructose corn syrup, sugar is found in everything from crackers to canned beans. Sugar prevents the hormone in your brain from telling you to stop eating, and so there's a tendency to feel hungry, even if you really aren't.

4 **Buy organic and humanely raised meats whenever possible.** Be aware that the conventionally grown produce in the grocery store has been fertilized with chemicals and sprayed with pesticides and some has been genetically modified to create a higher yield. To prevent these chemicals from entering your body, it's important to buy organic whenever possible. And avoid conventional meat that has been pumped full of antibiotics. You'll want to opt for organic and humanely raised meats, too.

5 **Be kind to your body.** Eat five to six times throughout the day and drink lots of water—around eight 8-ounce glasses per day. Eating three small meals a day and two to three snacks keeps your metabolism going and your body feeling satisfied and full of energy. Sometimes you may think you are hungry, but you really are just thirsty. Water is key to keeping your body functioning properly, so stay hydrated.

Why Choose to Eat Clean?

Clean eating is about feeding yourself the highest quality ingredients to help your body perform its best. The foods we eat help build muscle, maintain a healthy immune system, and protect our organs. With clean eating, you'll feel good about what you put in your body—lots of fresh fruit and vegetables, lean proteins, and whole grains—and you'll see the results. By eating a diet that's considered clean, you'll have improved digestion, increased energy, and a reduced risk for disease, according to a 2013 study published by *Nutrition Reviews*.

While eating clean involves cooking many things from scratch and buying organic, with a little planning and smart shopping, you can make this lifestyle work for you, no matter the size of your paycheck or how busy your schedule. Another great perk of eating clean? Your meals will be hearty enough to fill you up, but you'll probably lose weight due to the overall healthier content of the foods you're eating.

Say Good-Bye to Counting Calories

Clean eating is not a restrictive diet, so there is no need to count calories. It just makes sense that, since you're not eating the empty calories that processed foods deliver, you'll be consuming the proper amount of calories that whole foods inherently offer. An added bonus is that most clean foods simply aren't high in calories. Even the ones that are slightly higher in calories—such as avocados and olive oil—contain "good" fat, so there is a benefit they confer.

When you start looking at the recipes in this book, you'll notice that they include nutritional information, including calorie counts. If you're used to counting calories, it might be comforting to have this information, at least in the beginning, to be able to compare what you get from clean foods versus diets you've tried previously. As you start to feel better and better as a clean eater, the compulsion to count calories will correspondingly decrease.

Clean eaters don't have a free pass, however, to eat as much as they'd like. Keeping portions appropriately sized is important. Each day, you should eat roughly six to ten servings of complex carbohydrates, five to six servings of lean protein, and two to three servings of heart-healthy fats. But what exactly is a "serving"?

- 1 serving of whole grains = your cupped palm (½ cup)
- 1 serving of vegetables = your fist or both palms cupped together (1 cup)
- 1 serving of lean protein = the flat palm of your hand (3 ounces)
- 1 serving of fat = the top half of your thumb (1 teaspoon)
- 1 serving of cheese = your thumb (1 ounce)
- 1 serving of nuts or seeds = ½ of your cupped palm (¼ cup)

By eating the right foods in proper portions, your metabolism will keep going and you won't consume more than you should. Remember to eat slowly, to savor every bite, and to eat until you're satisfied instead of eating until you're "full."

Clean Up
Digestion

FOODS FOR A HEALTHY BELLY

One of the many benefits to eating clean is that it promotes good digestive health. Fill your plate with these clean eating stars:

Beans, whole grains, and berries: Each is high in fiber, which promotes good digestion.

Fermented foods: These foods contain beneficial bacteria that aid in digestion. Whether it's sauerkraut, buttermilk, sourdough, kefir (fermented milk), kimchi (fermented vegetables), or miso (fermented soybeans), they promote healthy bacteria in the digestive tract while adding a punch of flavor to your meal.

Ginger: This age-old remedy for tummy troubles speeds up the process of food moving from the stomach to the upper small intestine.

Water: By staying hydrated, your body's water works with fiber to move solids easily through your system.

Yogurt: Filled with good bacteria, live cultures, and probiotics, plain yogurt is a good choice to keep your digestion functioning well.

Clean Foods

A good way to ensure that you obtain clean whole foods is to buy mostly fresh ingredients that you will find around the perimeter of the grocery store. That is where you'll find the produce, meat, fresh fish, dairy, and freshly baked bread. You can then supplement with whole grains, beans, and frozen items.

Fresh fruit and vegetables: When possible, buy organic produce, with the possible exception of the "Clean 15" (a list of 15 conventionally grown fruits and vegetables with the lowest levels of pesticides; see page 316 for specifics). If you choose pre-chopped vegetables or fruit, be sure there aren't any added ingredients.

Herbs and spices: For spice blends, choose pure and organic blends without any added sodium or sugar. Italian seasoning, for example, should only include dried herbs like thyme, basil, and oregano.

Dairy: Buy organic milk, cheese, and yogurt whenever possible. Choose unsweetened varieties of yogurt. If you're limiting dairy products or just want to try something different, unsweetened coconut milk, almond milk, and rice milk are healthy options. Also use organic butter or organic spread and steer clear of margarine, imitation butter, whipped, and spreadable butter as they contain chemicals or fillers. Check the label to make sure there are no unclean ingredients.

Whole grains: For whole-grain products, make sure the label says 100 percent whole wheat or whole grain to ensure that the entire grain is used. If not, there's a good chance unclean ingredients are present.

Nuts and seeds: These delicious natural foods are perfect for tossing on salads or enjoying as a snack because they are made of heart-healthy fats that can help reduce cholesterol. Preferably, buy unsalted or low-salt nuts and make sure they aren't sweetened.

Dried fruit: From dried figs to dried cranberries, these sweet fruits can satisfy your sweet tooth in a healthy way. Choose unsweetened fruit and those without sulfites, which is often added as a preservative to extend shelf life.

Lean meats: Stick to lean cuts of meat for lower amounts of saturated fat. Buy organic meats, too, to avoid consuming hormones and pesticides that the animal may have been exposed to. These pesticides linger in animal fat, so buying lean cuts of conventionally raised meat reduces your chance of consuming them.

Clean oils: Coconut oil and avocado oil are suggested for cooking because their chemical structures don't break down when exposed to high heat. Extra-virgin olive oil and unrefined nut oils are more sensitive to heat, so these oils are ideal for salad dressings to take advantage of their heart-healthy benefits.

Legumes: It's safest to use natural, dried beans. But in a pinch, it's okay to buy canned beans for making quick meals. For guidelines on buying canned foods, jump to the bottom of this page.

Sweeteners: There are many clean eating options for sweeteners, including honey, maple syrup, organic evaporated cane juice, coconut sugar, and liquid stevia. Organic evaporated cane juice resembles coarse sugar and is closest to the unprocessed natural sugar cane plant so it contains more nutrients than processed sugar. And because it's organic, there are no pesticides, either. Coconut sugar is made from the sap of the coconut palm flower buds. This sugar is thought to be more nutritious than cane sugar and has a lower glycemic index (causes a smaller spike in blood sugar). Another natural sweetener to try is liquid stevia. Stevia is a plant, and the leaves are sweet. Liquid stevia is the extract from these leaves and has a negligible effect on blood glucose. However, avoid powdered stevia. While many packages say that it's "pure" or "organic," it is chemically processed and most versions include other ingredients like dextrose.

Canned and Frozen Foods

It's easy to understand why so many people gravitate toward prepared foods, given the time savings they afford. If you're short on time, it's absolutely fine to buy pre-chopped vegetables, frozen produce, and canned beans. Just be sure there aren't any problem additives hiding in the ingredients list.

A Closer Look
Coconut Oil

A MULTITUDE OF HEALTH BENEFITS

You'll find this oil in a significant amount of recipes throughout the book. Coconut is high in saturated fat, but because it is a naturally occurring saturated fat, as opposed to a hydrogenated trans fat, coconut oil can be appreciated for many health benefits. According to Joseph Mercola, MD, coconut oil can increase your metabolism, improve heart health, increase thyroid activity, maintain an ideal body weight, and improve your energy and immune system. It's an excellent cooking oil because it has a high smoke point. When other oils like olive oil are heated to high temperatures, the beneficial compounds of the oil actually start to degrade and can even create potentially harmful compounds. And no, coconut oil doesn't taste like coconuts. If you are concerned about saturated fat, use it occasionally and in small amounts, when you would normally use butter or canola oil.

A can of chopped tomatoes, for example, should have only one ingredient on the label. And make sure that cans are free of bisphenol A (BPA), too. BPA is found in the polybcarbonate plastics and epoxy resins used to coat the inside of metal cans and bottle tops. BPA can seep into food and could have potential harmful health effects on the brain and behavior. While the FDA has said that BPA is safe at very low levels, it is a good idea to avoid BPA products when possible. Look for products labeled BPA-free, and seek out glass containers when possible.

Sometimes in-season produce is cheaper fresh than frozen, but when it's out of season, frozen is a handy option. Look for organic and be careful to check the labels for lurking unnecessary or unclean ingredients. Frozen fruits are notorious for having added sugar. Stay away from packaging that says "in syrup" or "sweetened." With frozen vegetables, be on the lookout for blends flavored with a sauce. And, there could be sodium lurking there, too.

The Role of Gluten and Dairy in Clean Eating

Gluten and dairy products, in their purest form, are clean. But many people avoid eating them regardless, and it's important to understand why.

Gluten is a protein found in wheat and other grain products and is responsible for holding foods together. What makes wheat products unclean is the processing method they undergo that strips the wheat of its nutritional value. Gluten also serves as a thickener in other highly processed foods, such as sauces, soups, and everyday condiments ketchup and barbeque sauce. By avoiding gluten, one naturally removes from the diet many foods that have been processed. For some, however, cutting out gluten is not merely a lifestyle choice. Gluten sensitivity and gluten intolerance are real issues for many people, and it's often easiest for them to keep their digestive systems in balance by avoiding gluten and the products in which it's found. For those who don't have gluten sensitivity, be sure to buy the least processed grains available. Look for 100 percent whole-grain, sprouted-grain, or whole-wheat items for a clean eating approach, and when in doubt, check the label.

Lactose is a type of sugar naturally found in cow's milk and other dairy products. People need an enzyme in the small intestine, called lactase, to digest lactose. Babies and children have plenty of lactase but many adults, as many as 60 percent, no longer make enough of it. Lactose intolerance occurs when lactose cannot be digested. But not all dairy products have to be avoided. Yogurt, especially Greek yogurt, and kefir, which is a drinkable yogurt, have good live bacteria, called probiotics, which help digest the lactose. Also, hard cheeses such as Cheddar or Parmesan have no lactose since lactose is in the watery part of milk. It's best to avoid frozen yogurt, however, unless real yogurt is used. The label should having the wording "live, active cultures" or "probiotics" to let you know. While those who are lactose intolerant need to stay away from cow's milk, there are many easy-to-find, nutritious, and delicious alternatives available, such as almond milk, coconut milk, and soy milk.

With both gluten and dairy, listen to your body. Try various products and pay attention to how you feel after you've eaten them. And consult your physician if you have any questions about your body's reaction to foods.

Get to Know Unfamiliar Ingredients

Pretty soon, your pantry will transform into a clean eating pantry. For the most part, you will recognize all of the ingredients, but there are a few items that may be new to you. Here's a snapshot:

Grains and seeds: Farro, quinoa, barley, flaxseed, steel-cut oats, and chia seeds are all high-fiber and high-protein foods to add to your diet. In addition to helping you feel full and aiding your digestion, they are full of healthy vitamins and minerals.

Arrowroot powder: Also known as arrowroot starch, this natural product is an alternative to cornstarch or flour for thickening liquids. Cornstarch is derived from corn grown with genetically modified organisms (GMOs), and the process to create cornstarch involves using chemicals to transform corn into a powder. Arrowroot powder, on the other hand, is created by removing the starch from the plant's root by a mashing and filtering process.

Clean Up

Heart

Eating good fats and fresh foods promotes heart health. Mono-unsaturated fats help regulate insulin levels and blood sugar; polyunsaturated fats help keep cholesterol in check. Be sure to fill your shopping cart with these heart-friendly foods:

Apples: An apple a day can help reduce bad (LDL) cholesterol.

Cruciferous vegetables: Veggies in the cabbage family, like broccoli, cauliflower, cabbage, and kale, reduce inflammation, are packed with antioxidants, and are high in fiber.

Extra-virgin olive oil: This first-press oil helps unclog arteries.

Green tea: This soothing drink is packed with antioxidants that help reduce blood clots.

Salmon: Packed with omega-3 fatty acids, this fish is a great protein choice.

Sweet potatoes, oranges, and red bell peppers: These foods are high in vitamin C, which helps protect against aging and stroke, and reduces cholesterol.

Sprouted-grain products: Sprouted-grain bread products are some of the best you can consume, and contain easy-to-digest whole grains. The grains are sprouted by being soaked in water, and this process releases enzymes that break down proteins and carbo-hydrates, making the bread easy to digest and low on the glycemic index. The nutrients from the grains are also absorbed immediately instead of being lost during the digestive process.

Tamari and coconut aminos: These condiments are natural products recommended for clean eating flavorings instead of soy sauce. Soy sauce is a highly processed product and often contains hidden amounts of wheat gluten. Tamari is a Japanese-style soy sauce that is often made as a byproduct of miso. You'll want to look for organic tamari made with non-GMO soy beans and no gluten. Check the label to make sure the product adheres to clean eating principles. Coconut aminos is made from coconut tree sap and sea salt and is naturally aged. It contains no soy or gluten while still imparting a soy sauce–like flavor to foods.

Unclean Foods

With some foods, it's easy to tell that they are unclean and should be avoided. Candy bars, potato chips, soda, and artificial sweeteners are clear examples. But with other foods, it's not so easy to decipher which category they belong in.

Low-fat, sugar-free, and fat-free: Don't be fooled by foods labeled low-fat, fat-free, or even gluten-free without reading the label. These foods have likely been supplemented with unclean ingredients to make up for flavor lost in the production process.

White foods: Stay away from "white" foods: white bread, white rice, granulated sugar. White flour and white rice, for example, have been stripped of all their healthy brown parts, so opt for whole grains instead. White sugar is highly refined, so turn to the list of clean sweeteners in this book, which will help you satisfy your sweet tooth in a healthy way.

Refined flour and sugars: To keep processed foods shelf stable, they have to be highly refined, and during this process, most or all of the nutrition has often been removed. Also look out for "enriched" or "fortified" foods. In these cases, vitamins and nutrients are added to refined products along with other unhealthy additives to fool us into thinking they are healthy, but they're not.

Nonclean oils: Canola oil, corn oil, vegetable oil, palm oil, soybean oil, and any hydrogenated oils are all highly processed and should be avoided.

Processed and packaged foods: Often times, these products contain processed sugars, unhealthy fats, and harmful chemicals to increase shelf life.

The role of corn in a clean eating diet is worth addressing head-on. Most of the corn products in supermarkets today are made with genetically modified organisms (GMOs), which places them squarely on the no-eating list for clean eaters. Unfortunately, there is no requirement for manufacturers to note on food labels that corn has been altered with GMOs. The only way to ensure you're buying non-GMO corn is to buy organic, whether it's fresh corn, tortilla chips, or polenta.

Taking Inventory

Now that you know the basics of eating clean, the next step is to take some time and think about your current eating habits. A great tool to have is a food journal. Before beginning the meal plan included in this book, you may want to write down what you eat over the course of a few days as well as how you felt afterward. Establish a baseline before you make the changes to eat clean. Over the next month, record what you eat, even if they are less-than-ideal choices. Remember that eating clean is a lifestyle choice, not a diet. It's absolutely fine, now and again, if you indulge with a cheeseburger or a piece of cake. In a few weeks, you'll look back and see how far you have come, and you'll feel empowered and proud of how well you're taking care of yourself.

Preparing to Eat Clean

Are you almost ready for your kick-off trip to the grocery store? Before you head out, give a once-over to your current pantry and do some spring cleaning (regardless of the season). After you know what you have at home, follow the tips in this chapter to find out what to buy to restock your pantry, and what to toss.

Have a Plan

The best way to succeed with a lifestyle change is to have a plan that you can stick to. The four-week clean eating meal plan set forth in detail in chapter 3 takes the guesswork out of grocery shopping by equipping you with a complete shopping list for all the meals of each week. That way, you know exactly what to buy and use for cooking, and you won't end up with a refrigerator (or compost bin) full of unused ingredients. You'll also learn what to prep ahead and how to stock a clean eating pantry. Best of all, you'll find tips on how to save precious time and money. After four weeks of following this meal plan, you'll be a clean eating pro, likely doing all you can to hold yourself back from evangelizing about it to friends and family.

If you are new to following a meal plan, this book includes step-by-step instructions for how to make shopping and preparing meals fun and easy. The first step is to start with an open mind and to go easy on yourself. It may take a day or even a week or two on the meal plan to get used to eating clean. The meal plan is there to guide you in making healthy choices, and pretty soon you will be on your way to a healthier lifestyle. To help you get started, we've included the following elements in this book:

A Weekly Menu: At the beginning of each week of the four-week meal plan, you'll get a listing of the enticing dishes you'll be eating for every meal and snack over the next seven days. The meal plan includes innovative ways of using the fresh ingredients for that week, simply supplemented with items in your pantry, so that by the end of the week you will have used that week's purchases in preparing meals. You won't have wilted, unused food to toss, and the fridge will be ready for restocking for the next week.

A Grocery Shopping List: There's a shopping list for each week, which includes all of the ingredients you will need for the seven days of meals. The list includes the fresh items as well as those you should find in your pantry.

Prep Ahead Tips: Many of the recipes can be made ahead and stored for convenience. There's a list at the end of each week that will help you plan ahead to save time during the next busy week.

Worry-Free Meal Plan: Breakfast, lunch, dinner, and dessert are planned out for you. You can choose from 12 snacks to enjoy when you'd like. These include clean eating ready-made snacks you can find at the grocery store as well as recipes to make and store some snacks when you have free time.

Twice as Nice: Several of the recipes are intended to generate leftovers that are reinvented later in the week to help you save time and money.

Clean Condiments: Sauces, dressings, and other condiments that meet clean eating standards are commonly troublesome to find, so there's a bonus chapter at the end of the book with recipes for

Is It Clean?
Flour

KNOW WHAT TO LOOK FOR

For all you bread lovers out there, the good news is that you can find clean flour. But look carefully. The Whole Grains Council describes the milling process and recommends what to look for when buying grain products: Whole-wheat flour contains the entire wheat berry, minus the inedible husk. When "whole" is taken out of the equation, you are left with highly processed, most likely bleached, milled-wheat flour that is missing essentially all of the nutrition. Bye-bye, all-purpose flour. Only purchase 100 percent whole-wheat or whole-grain flour to know, without a doubt, that it's clean. Also look for quinoa flour, brown rice flour, and almond meal flour to expand your clean alternative options.

Is It Clean?
Peanut Butter

CHECK THE LABEL FOR CLEAN INGREDIENTS

Finding a clean eating peanut butter can be tricky. The easiest thing to do is check the label on the jar. Does it say organic? Does it include only peanuts in the ingredients and perhaps a little bit of salt? Conventional jarred peanut butter is often pumped with high-fructose corn syrup, extra sodium, and hydrogenated oil, which are unnecessary and actually destroy the wonderful fresh taste of natural, ground peanuts. These days, you can more easily find clean eating peanut butter at your local grocery store. Or better yet, turn to the recipe for Creamy Natural Peanut Butter on page 306 and make your own. And remember, other nutritious alternatives to peanut butter are almond butter and cashew butter.

making your favorites like ketchup, salad dressing, peanut butter, and barbecue sauce.

Party of Two, Four, or More: Most of the recipes in the book serve four people. If you are a couple starting the meal plan, the recipes easily can be divided in half. Or, if your family is larger than four, the recipes can simply be doubled. You'll also find helpful freezing and storage tips for leftovers.

Reading Food Labels

The easiest way to follow a clean diet is to buy ingredients that don't require a label—apples or oranges, for example. But let's be honest. Every now and again you'll get a craving for a food item and it is not time efficient to make your own. There are some great, healthy options in the center aisles of the grocery store like whole grains that you'll want to include. You just have to read the labels.

Here is a typical Nutrition Facts food label (see figure, right).

Check the serving size first. Sometimes serving sizes are much less than what someone would typically eat. If you intend to eat two servings, be sure to multiply each of the calories, fat, sodium, and so on, by two.

A category to pay particular close attention to is the fat category, which includes total fat, saturated fat, and trans fat. You'll want to limit excess fat in your diet, and when you fill your meals with vegetables and fruits, that will become easier. As mentioned earlier, monounsaturated and polyunsaturated fats are actually good for you. Look out for saturated fats and trans fats that raise bad cholesterol. Saturated fats (from animal products) should be consumed in small amounts. Trans fats should be avoided completely: They are commercially processed fats designed to

Nutrition Facts

Serving Size 1 cup (110g)
Servings Per Container About 6

Amount Per Serving

Calories 250 — Calories from Fat 30

	% Daily Value*
Total Fat 7g	11%
Saturated Fat 3g	16%
Trans Fat 0g	
Cholesterol 4mg	2%
Sodium 300mg	13%
Total Carbohydrate 30g	10%
Dietary Fiber 3g	14%
Sugars 2g	
Protein 5g	

Vitamin A	7%
Vitamin C	15%
Calcium	20%
Iron	32%

* Percent Daily Values are based on a 2,000 calorie diet. Your daily value may be higher or lower depending on your calorie needs.

	Calories:	2,000	2,500
Total Fat	Less than	55g	75g
Saturated Fat	Less than	10g	12g
Cholesterol	Less than	1,500mg	1,700mg
Total Carbohydrate		250mg	300mg
Dietary Fiber		22mg	31mg

increase shelf life and make liquid vegetable oils solid at room temperature.

With vitamins and minerals, you'll want to get the highest percentage of your daily allowance as possible. Look for fiber content: Foods high in fiber also help keep you full longer.

Generally, remember to check the food labels to make sure you know what you are putting in your body. If a recipe calls for 100 percent whole-wheat pasta, check the label and make sure there are not unclean ingredients like enriched flour. Sugar, used as a preservative, is another ingredient that sneaks its way into foods. Sucrose, fructose, glucose, high-fructose corn syrup, and dextrose are all sugar. Sodium is salt. Packaged and canned foods often contain large amounts of sodium for flavor.

Shopping Tips

One of the biggest concerns with beginning a clean eating plan is the cost of fresh fruits and vegetables and the time it takes to go to the store. With a little planning and smart shopping, however, this lifestyle doesn't break the bank or take up all your free time.

Shop the perimeter of the grocery store. The outer rim of the grocery store is where most of your clean eating foods are shelved: fresh produce, lean meats, and dairy. This is also where you won't find many labels, so you can grab your ingredients quickly, and search Nutritional Facts in the center aisles.

Buy produce in season. Not only does produce taste better when it's in season, it's also usually cheaper. Seasonal produce also probably hasn't traveled across the country or across the ocean to get to your grocery store. When in doubt, turn to page 314 for a list of when specific fruits and vegetables are at their peak.

Shop at your local farmers' market. Your local farmers' market is the perfect way to stock up on the freshest produce. You know it's from your area and it was probably picked just that morning. Not only are you helping your family eat healthily, but you're also helping promote local farming practices. Another benefit is you can

Is It Clean?
Soy Sauce

SAVORY SUBSTITUTES ARE THE BEST BET

While soy sauce used to be made by boiling soybeans and then fermenting them in salt for several months, the process has changed. Nowadays, it's cheaper and less time-consuming to take a few shortcuts, and these new methods are what make soy sauce something to avoid. Modern soy sauce is pasteurized, killing all of the bacteria created during the fermentation process. These bacteria are most likely beneficial for our health, but killing them allows the soy sauce to be shelf stable for months or even years. The current process used to speed the fermentation process is called acid-hydrolysis. The proteins are removed with hydrochloric acid, and coloring and flavoring are added in their place. Another ingredient frequently added to the soy sauce is highly processed wheat. But don't be discouraged if you love the umami—or savory—flavor of soy sauce. Tamari and coconut aminos (see page 31) are great substitutes for this favorite Asian condiment.

talk directly to the farmer to learn more about the specifics of the produce and make sure it is organic (or if it's one of the Clean 15). Many cities also have co-ops with baskets of organic produce ready for pickup each week. This is a convenient way to get in your fruits and vegetables.

Never shop hungry. If you walk into the grocery store with a growling stomach, you'll be more susceptible to grabbing unhealthy foods. Instead, always be prepared with a snack in your purse to calm your hunger before shopping.

Come to the store with a list. Like shopping on an empty stomach, coming to the store without a list can lead to unclean ingredients ending up in your cart. After you've gone through the four-week meal plan this book offers and gotten used to making your own meal plans and sticking to the shopping lists, you'll have a much easier time sticking to clean eating all the time.

Opt for protein alternatives. Organic meats and seafood can be expensive. By supplementing with a mixture of vegetarian dishes, with beans and other protein alternatives, both your appetite and your wallet will be satisfied.

Buy in bulk whenever possible. Take advantage of your grocery store's weekly sales on various items and buy organic meat when it's marked down. Place what you don't need in zip-top plastic freezer bags with the name and date. When you're ready to use the ingredient, let it thaw in the refrigerator overnight.

Know what to buy organic. Ideally, it's best to cook with all organic produce, but sometimes that's not possible. The Environmental Working Group has created lists known as the "Dirty Dozen" and the "Clean 15." The Dirty Dozen consists of the fruits and vegetables that are conventionally treated with a lot of pesticides or readily absorb the chemicals, and that's why they're considered dirty. Those items should always be bought organic. The Clean 15 refers to fruits and vegetables that are conventionally treated with very low amounts of pesticide and/or don't absorb the chemicals as deeply, so you can opt not to buy the organic versions of these if an organic option is unavailable or too pricey. Regardless of whether you purchase conventional produce or organic, always thoroughly wash it before eating. See appendix C (page 316) for the complete Dirty Dozen and Clean 15 list.

Essential Tools and Equipment

Every kitchen should be stocked with certain basic cooking equipment, like measuring cups and spoons, spatulas, wooden spoons, a box grater or hand grater, and a vegetable peeler. These will be used in the recipes in this book. But beyond the basics, here's what else you should have available for cooking:

Knives: A good chef's knife, paring knife, and serrated knife are all must-haves in the kitchen. For each tool, choose the best quality you can afford and make sure it feels good in your hand.

Rimmed baking sheet: Choose a light-colored baking sheet and be sure it's heavy duty so it can withstand high temperatures for roasting vegetables. A 10-by-15-inch baking sheet is a versatile size.

Wire-mesh strainer: This tool can double as a colander if it's big enough. Pay attention to the size of the holes. If you only have a large-holed strainer, small items like grains or beans could fall through.

Tongs: Tongs can act as an extension of your hand, and they are necessary for grilling. Choose a spring-loaded model for ease of use.

Kitchen shears: Kitchen scissors can serve many utilitarian uses in the kitchen: They can snip fresh herbs, open containers, chop tomatoes in the can, and cut meat into bite-size pieces. Dishwasher-safe shears that separate are the most convenient.

Steamer basket: Steaming vegetables helps them retain more nutrients than boiling, and this gadget is great for quickly cooking portions of fresh veggies. Look for a collapsible basket with sturdy handles for ease of use.

Nonstick skillet: Using a nonstick skillet reduces the need for fats and oils while helping prevent food from sticking. If you are con-

Clean Up
Brain

You don't have to be a rocket scientist—or a professor of neurosurgery, like UCLA's Fernando Gómez-Pinilla—to know that food can affect brain function. But it doesn't hurt that brain scientists such as Gómez-Pinilla are publishing research that confirms that foods high in omega-3 fatty acids and antioxidants have a positive effect on brain health. Make sure your shopping cart often includes these brain-happy foods:

Avocados: Avocados are great for more than guacamole. They contribute to healthy blood flow, vascular health, and keep the brain young.

Beets: These root vegetables are a great source of nitrates that promote blood and oxygen flow to the brain.

Berries: Blueberries, raspberries, strawberries, and other berries help protect from oxidative stress and aid with memory and focus. Eat one cup a day to help prevent Alzheimer's disease and dementia.

Nuts: Packed with vitamin E and healthy fats, nuts help regulate blood flow and keep oxygen going to the brain. They are also thought to reduce cognitive decline and are filled with anti-inflammatory nutrients.

Salmon: Rich in omega-3 fatty acids, salmon enhances brain function and contains anti-inflammatory properties. It is also believed to improve focus and memory, and lower the risk of dementia. Be sure to enjoy natural wild salmon two to three times a week.

Spinach and leafy greens: The antioxidant lutein found in these green veggies is thought to protect against cognitive decline.

Water: When you are dehydrated your brain actually shrinks. Keeping hydrated keeps cognitive function at its best.

cerned with the chemicals often found in nonstick pan coating, there are several eco-friendly cookware brands that are PFOA- and PTFE-free. PFOA in high doses has been found to be carcinogenic in lab tests. Remember to use silicone or wood utensils with nonstick pans so you don't scratch the coating.

Grill: Don't worry if you don't have an outdoor propane or charcoal grill. A table-top grill press, like a Foreman grill, works well, or you can use a skillet for grilling by covering meat or vegetables with foil and placing a saucepan filled with heavy canned goods on top.

Dutch oven: This heavy-duty pot makes easy work of creating soups, stews, and braised dishes. Be sure to buy one that is oven-safe with a tight-fitting lid to lock moisture in.

Large (2- to 3-quart) saucepan: A large saucepan is very useful in the kitchen. It can be used for small-batch soups, sauces, and even vegetables and side dishes. Choose one with comfortable handles and a tight-fitting lid for versatility.

Stockpot: A stockpot with at least an 8-quart capacity is ideal for boiling pasta or making other large-batch dishes.

Other Helpful Equipment

Slow cooker: These small appliances can be lifesavers when you have a busy day. Recipes that call for using slow cookers often have quick prep times so you can put all of the ingredients in the crock before you leave in the morning and let the slow cooker do the work while you're away. A 5- to 6-quart slow cooker is a good size for general use and is the most versatile with recipes.

Rice cooker: This gadget is an effortless way to make steamed rice and other steamed grains and is extremely convenient to have. Simply measure out the rice and water per the manufacturer's instructions, turn on the rice cooker, put on the lid, and press the button, while you proceed with preparing the rest of your meal. The rice cooker automatically turns itself off when the rice is perfectly done and keeps it warm.

3

Week-by-Week Clean Eating Meal Plans

Designed with you and your busy schedule in mind, this four-week clean eating meal plan takes the guesswork out of planning meals, grocery shopping, and preparing meals.

Each week has its own menu plan, suggested recipes, list of pantry items, amounts you will use, and a specific shopping list. At the end of each week, you'll find some "Prep Ahead" tips for the following week to help you get meals on the table quickly.

Week One

Welcome to your first week of clean eating. This week you will put into practice the fundamental principle of the diet: You'll eat lots of fresh fruits and vegetables, lean protein, and whole grains. As you make this lifestyle change, remember to keep these two guidelines in mind:

1 **Train your taste buds:** This first week, you may find that you have a craving for something sweet. Instead of reaching for a box of cookies, try some fresh fruit or the Chocolate-Almond Dip with Strawberries (page 151). You are beginning to train your taste buds to enjoy natural sugars from fruits instead of artificial ones found in processed foods, and it may take a couple of weeks to get there.

2 **Learn to eat all day long:** To keep your metabolism going and keep hunger at bay, you will be eating five to six times a day. This may be a big adjustment, so keep snacks prepared and handy—in a portable cooler, on your desk, or in your car—so that you always have a clean eating snack to satisfy you until the next meal.

Week One Menu at a Glance

DAY ONE

Breakfast Streusel-Topped Blueberry Muffins
Lunch Mediterranean Turkey Wrap
Dinner Spice-Rubbed Salmon with Citrus Salsa and Steamed Green Beans
Dessert Dark Cherry, Pistachio, Coconut, and Bittersweet Chocolate Bark

DAY TWO

Breakfast Triple-Berry Smoothie
Lunch Almond Butter–Apple Sandwiches
Dinner Braised Pork Loin with Dried Figs and Roasted Asparagus
Dessert Broiled Grapefruit with Honeyed Yogurt

DAY THREE

Breakfast Pumpkin-Pecan Breakfast Cookies
Lunch Three-Bean Farro Salad
Dinner Curried Chickpeas with Spinach and Brown Rice
Dessert Quick Vanilla Pudding

DAY FOUR

Breakfast Spinach–Red Pepper Frittata with Feta
Lunch Turkey-Cucumber Sandwich with Mashed Avocado
Dinner Peanut Noodles with Shredded Pork and Vegetables
(use leftover pork from Day Two)
Dessert Fudgy Chocolate Chunk–Pecan Brownies

DAY FIVE

Breakfast Tropical Smoothie
Lunch Creamy Asparagus Soup
Dinner Grilled Honey-Mustard Chicken with Marinated
Tomatoes and Cucumbers
Dessert Strawberry Shortcakes

DAY SIX

Breakfast Eggs Baked in Toast Cups
Lunch Chicken-Quinoa Salad with Oranges, Olives, and Feta
Dinner Grilled Mini Veggie Pizzas
Dessert Frozen Blueberry-Granola Bars

DAY SEVEN

Breakfast Scrambled Egg, Black Bean, and Avocado Breakfast
Burritos
Lunch Curried Vegetable Soup
Dinner Chicken Breasts Stuffed with Roasted Red Peppers,
Olives, and Feta
Dessert Apple Crumble

Weekly Snacks

Choose one or two each day.

1. Apple slices with almond butter
2. Orange slices and a handful of whole almonds
3. Trail mix of nuts and dried fruit (no added sugar)
4. Nitrate-free turkey breast
5. Cucumber slices topped with fresh basil and feta cheese
6. Greek yogurt and ¼ cup fresh blueberries
7. Tomato wedges drizzled with balsamic vinegar
8. Handful of shelled pistachios
9. Fresh Salsa* with 100% whole-grain tortilla chips
10. Chocolate-Almond Dip with Strawberries*
11. Crunchy Cumin-Spiced Chickpeas*
12. Roasted Carrot Dip* with Herbed Pita Chips*

Recipe included in recipe section

Week One Pantry

OILS AND VINEGARS

- Oil, avocado
- Oil, coconut
- Oil, extra-virgin olive
- Vinegar, balsamic
- Vinegar, white wine

HERBS AND SPICES

- Allspice
- Bay leaves
- Cinnamon, ground
- Cumin, ground
- Curry powder
- Mustard, dried
- Nutmeg, ground
- Pepper, black
- Salt
- Smoked paprika
- Red pepper flakes, crushed
- Thyme, dried

SWEETENERS

- Cane juice, evaporated
- Coconut sugar
- Honey
- Maple syrup

FLOURS AND GRAINS

- Farro
- Flour, 100% whole-wheat pastry
- Oats, rolled
- Pasta, 100% whole-grain linguine
- Pasta, 100% whole-wheat orzo
- Quinoa, dry
- Rice, brown

CONDIMENTS

- Hot sauce, sambal oelek chili
- Mustard, Dijon
- Mustard, grainy Dijon
- Tamari or coconut aminos

DRIED FRUIT AND NUT BUTTERS

- Apricots, unsweetened
- Almond butter, all-natural
- Cherries, unsweetened
- Cranberries, unsweetened
- Figs, unsweetened

NUTS AND SEEDS

- Almond extract
- Almonds, dry-roasted
- Flaxseed
- Peanuts, dry-roasted
- Pecans, chopped
- Pistachios, unsalted shelled
- Pumpkin seeds

OTHER

- Arrowroot powder
- Baking powder
- Baking soda
- Chocolate, 70% bittersweet
- Cocoa powder, unsweetened
- Coconut, unsweetened shredded
- Olives, green, pitted
- Olives, Kalamata, pitted
- Peppers, red, roasted
- Pumpkin, canned unsweetened
- Vanilla extract, pure

Week One Shopping List

VEGETABLES

- Asparagus (5½ pounds)
- Avocados (2)
- Baby spinach, fresh (three 11-ounce clamshells)
- Carrots (2 pounds)
- Cucumbers (4)
- Green beans, fresh (2½ pounds)
- Jalapeño peppers (2)
- Onions, red, large (6)
- Squash, yellow and zucchini, pre-sliced, frozen (two 12-ounce bags)
- Tomatoes (4)
- Vegetables, stir-fry mix, without sauce, frozen (one 16-ounce package)

HERBS AND SPICES

- Basil (1 bunch)
- Cilantro (2 bunches)
- Garlic cloves (2 heads)
- Ginger (3-inch piece)

GRAINS

- Bread, sprouted-grain, frozen (2 loaves)
- Tortillas, sprouted or 100% whole-grain (eight 6-inch)

FRUIT

- Apples (7)
- Berries, mixed, frozen (one 48-ounce bag)
- Blueberries (2 pints)
- Grapefruit, ruby red (4)
- Lemons (2)
- Limes (5)
- Oranges (7)
- Pineapple, chunks, frozen (one 16-ounce bag)
- Strawberries (1 quart)

MEAT AND FISH

- Chicken breasts, boneless, skinless (11)
- Pork, cooked, shredded (1 pound)
- Pork, loin roast, boneless (3½ pounds)
- Salmon fillets, skinless (4)
- Turkey, deli-roasted, sliced (1 pound)

EGGS AND DAIRY

- Butter (2 sticks)
- Cheese, Cheddar, white (6 ounces)
- Cheese, feta (8 ounces)
- Eggs (2 dozen)
- Milk (24 ounces)
- Yogurt, Greek, plain (two 32-ounce containers)

OTHER

- Beans, black (one 15-ounce can)
- Beans, kidney (one 15-ounce can)
- Broth, chicken, reduced-sodium (one 14.5-ounce can)
- Broth, vegetable, reduced-sodium (one 32-ounce can)
- Chickpeas (three 15-ounce cans)
- Tomatoes, stewed (one 14.5-ounce can)
- Tomatoes, whole in puree (two 28-ounce cans)

Prep Ahead

On the weekend or when you find free time, make these recipes ahead of time to help you out during the following week:

- **Homemade Marinara Sauce** (page 294)
- **Pumpkin-Pecan Breakfast Cookies** (page 95)
- **Crunchy Cumin-Spiced Chickpeas** (page 136)

Week Two

You've made it to week two! By now, you're getting used to clean eating and trading out some of those not-so-clean ingredients and replacing them with more healthy ones. This week, think about these guidelines:

1. **Don't forget to drink lots of water:** When schedules get busy and hectic, it may be hard to remember to reach for that water glass. To help you get in your eight (8-ounce) glasses, a day, keep a large glass water bottle constantly by your side. One that has an ounce marker on the side makes it easier to keep track of how much water you have consumed during the day.

2. **De-clutter the pantry:** You may notice that your pantry is getting cramped if you still have unclean items lurking about. Do a good deed and donate canned goods and packaged items that have not yet expired to your local food bank, and you'll make some extra space on the shelves for your clean eating items.

Week Two Menu at a Glance

DAY ONE

Breakfast Hash Brown Scramble
Lunch Southwestern Salad with Shrimp and Black Beans
Dinner Slow-Cooked Italian Pot Roast and Vegetables
Dessert Carrot Cake Cupcakes

DAY TWO

Breakfast Almond, Cherry, and Vanilla Smoothie
Lunch Corn and Potato Chowder
Dinner Mushroom Barley Risotto
Dessert Lemon-Lime Granita

DAY THREE

Breakfast Nutty Whole-Grain Waffles
Lunch Pasta Salad with Avocado-Pesto Cream Sauce
Dinner Lemon-Garlic Roasted Chicken with Steamed Broccoli and Wild Rice
Dessert Yogurt Cheesecake Bars with Berry Topping

DAY FOUR

Breakfast Slow Cooker Overnight Oatmeal with Fresh Cherries and Maple Syrup
Lunch Chicken-Pesto BLT (use leftover Lemon-Garlic Chicken)
Dinner Shredded Beef Tacos (use leftover Pot Roast from Day One)
Dessert Amaretti Cookies

DAY FIVE

Breakfast Avocado-Lime Smoothie
Lunch Tuna-Barley Salad with Roasted Red Peppers and Artichokes
Dinner Grilled Portobello Burgers with Sweet Potato Fries
Dessert Dark Chocolate Bread Puddings

DAY SIX

Breakfast Streusel-Topped Blueberry Muffins (defrost from Week One)
Lunch Minestrone Soup (double to have leftovers for Week Three)
Dinner Thai Shrimp and Snow Pea Curry
Dessert Yogurt Cheesecake Bars with Berry Topping (from Day Three)

DAY SEVEN

Breakfast Mango Lassi Smoothie
Lunch Beef and Goat Cheese Quesadilla (uses leftover Pot Roast from Day One)
Dinner Chicken Pasta Puttanesca
Dessert Fudgy Chocolate Chunk–Pecan Brownies (defrost from Week One)

Weekly Snacks

Choose one or two each day.

1. Fresh cherries and white Cheddar cheese
2. Hard-boiled egg
3. Dried fruit chips
4. Sliced avocado on toasted sprouted-grain bread
5. A small box of raisins
6. Air-popped organic popcorn
7. A handful of cashews
8. Blue cheese–stuffed dates
9. All-natural granola bars
10. Sweet and Spicy Nuts*
11. Creamy Spinach-Artichoke Dip*
12. White Bean Hummus*

Recipe included in recipe section

Week Two Pantry

OILS AND VINEGARS

- Oil, avocado
- Oil, coconut
- Oil, extra-virgin olive
- Vinegar, balsamic
- Vinegar, white wine

HERBS AND SPICES

- Chili powder
- Cinnamon, ground
- Cloves, ground
- Cumin, ground
- Ginger, ground
- Herbes de Provence
- Oregano, dried
- Paprika, smoked
- Pepper, black
- Red pepper flakes, crushed
- Salt
- Thyme, dried

SWEETENERS

- Cane juice, evaporated
- Coconut sugar
- Honey
- Maple syrup, pure
- Stevia, liquid

FLOURS AND GRAINS

- Almond flour
- Barley
- Flour, 100% whole-wheat pastry
- Oats, rolled
- Oats, steel-cut
- Pasta, 100% whole-grain angel hair
- Pasta, 100% whole-grain elbow
- Pasta, 100% whole-grain fusilli
- Rice, brown
- Rice, wild

CONDIMENTS

- Curry paste, red
- Fish sauce
- Mustard, Dijon

NUTS AND SEEDS

- Almonds, sliced
- Flaxseed
- Pecans, chopped
- Pine nuts
- Walnuts

OTHER

- Almond extract
- Arrowroot powder
- Baking powder
- Baking soda
- Capers
- Chocolate, 70% bittersweet
- Cocoa powder, unsweetened
- Olives, Kalamata, pitted
- Peppers, red, roasted
- Vanilla extract, pure

Week Two Shopping List

VEGETABLES

- Avocado (6)
- Baby spinach, fresh
  (two 10-ounce bags)
- Broccoli (2 pounds)
- Carrots (2 pounds)
- Corn (5 ears)
- Jalapeño pepper (1)
- Lettuce, romaine (1 head)
- Mushrooms, portobello
  (2 pounds)
- Onions (6)
- Peas, frozen
  (one 10-ounce bag)
- Potatoes, new (1 pound)
- Snow peas, frozen
  (one 10-ounce bag)
- Sweet potatoes (4)
- Tomatoes (8)
- Zucchini (2)

HERBS AND SPICES

- Basil (2 bunches)
- Cilantro (1 bunch)
- Garlic cloves (2 heads)
- Ginger (3-inch piece)

GRAINS

- Tortillas, sprouted-grain
  or 100% whole-wheat
  (eight 6-inch)

FRUIT

- Cherries, pitted
  (1½ pounds)
- Lemons (5)
- Limes (5)
- Mango, chunks, frozen
  (one 16-ounce bag)

MEAT AND FISH

- Bacon, uncured (1 package)
- Chicken breasts, boneless,
  skinless (6)
- Chicken, whole
  (about 4 pounds)
- Beef, roast, eye-of-round
  (two 2-pound roasts)
- Beef, cooked, shredded
  (2 pounds)
- Shrimp, large, deveined and
  peeled (1½ pounds)

EGGS AND DAIRY

- Butter (2 sticks)
- Cheese, goat (4 ounces)
- Cheese, Cheddar, white (8 ounces)
- Cheese, Parmesan (8 ounces)
- Cream cheese (three 8-ounce blocks)
- Eggs (2 dozen)
- Milk (1 quart)
- Sour cream (one 28-ounce container)
- Yogurt, Greek, plain (one 32-ounce container)

OTHER

- Almond milk, unsweetened (48 ounces)
- Artichoke hearts, jarred (12 ounces)
- Beans, black (one 15-ounce can)
- Beans, kidney (one 15-ounce can)
- Broth, beef, reduced-sodium (one 14.5-ounce can)
- Broth, vegetable, reduced-sodium (three 32-ounce cartons)
- Coconut milk (two 13.5-ounce cans)
- Green chilis, roasted (one 4-ounce can)
- Hash browns, frozen (one 32-ounce bag)
- Tomatoes, diced (one 14.5-ounce can)
- Tomatoes, whole in puree (one 28-ounce can)
- Tomatoes, crushed in puree (one 28-ounce can)
- Tuna, albacore in water (two 5-ounce cans)

Prep Ahead

On the weekend or when you find you have free time, make these recipes ahead of time to help you out during the following week:

- **Slow-Cooked Italian Pot Roast and Vegetables** (page 258)
- **Basil Pesto** (page 292)
- **Sweet and Spicy Nuts** (page 134)

Week Three

Two weeks in, two weeks to go! Hopefully by now you are embracing the clean eating lifestyle and noticing some changes in your energy level and how you feel after you eat. Here are some principles to observe this week:

1   **Make it a family affair:** By now, the newness of clean eating may have worn off and you may be tempted to reach for unhealthy convenience items. Don't do it! Instead, have the family pitch in with the cooking, so you can all enjoy the new lifestyle. Have young children measure out ingredients or stir, and let your spouse do the chopping. When everyone is involved, mealtime can be fun.

2   **Prep ahead:** In addition to the prep suggestions at the end of each week, take a few minutes at the beginning of the week to go over the recipes you will be making. Many of the recipes can be worked on ahead of time. For example, you can chop vegetables in advance and place them in zip-top bags in the refrigerator. You can also make marinades and dressings ahead.

Week Three Menu at a Glance

DAY ONE

Breakfast Eggs Poached in Spiced Tomato Sauce
Lunch Black Bean Soup (make a large batch of Fresh Salsa for Week Four)
Dinner Shepherd's Pie
Dessert Amaretti Cookies (defrost dough from Week Two and bake)

DAY TWO

Breakfast Banana, Strawberry, and Walnut Smoothie
Lunch Mediterranean Turkey Wrap
Dinner Sausage, Lentil, and Kale Stew
Dessert Coconut Cream Pie

DAY THREE

Breakfast Mini Spinach, Pepper, and Cheese Quiches
Lunch Minestrone Soup
Dinner Flounder Piccata with Sun-Dried Tomato Rice Pilaf
Dessert Chocolate-Dipped Peppermint Meringues

DAY FOUR

Breakfast Baked Banana French Toast
Lunch Three-Bean Farro Salad (double Mustard-Thyme
Vinaigrette to use in Week Four)
Dinner Mini Meatloaves with Mashed Potatoes and Green Beans
Dessert Coconut Cream Pie (from Day Two)

DAY FIVE

Breakfast Ginger-Coconut Smoothie
Lunch Pasta Salad with Avocado-Pesto Cream Sauce (uses Basil
Pesto from Week Two)
Dinner Panko-Pecan Crusted Chicken Tenders with Steamed
Broccoli (uses Homemade Mayonnaise from Day Two)
Dessert Apple-Raisin Rice Pudding

DAY SIX

Breakfast South-of-the-Border Breakfast Strata (uses Fresh
Salsa from Day One)
Lunch Turkey-Cucumber Sandwiches with Mashed Avocado
Dinner Falafel Pitas with Tzatziki Sauce
Dessert Strawberry Shortcakes

DAY SEVEN

Breakfast Banana Nut Bread
Lunch Tuna-Barley Salad with Roasted Red Peppers
and Artichokes
Dinner Beet, Pear, and Mixed Greens Salad
Dessert Chocolate-Dipped Peppermint Meringues
(from Day Three)

Weekly Snacks

Choose one or two each day.

1. One banana
2. Greek yogurt topped with ½ cup sliced strawberries
3. Turkey, spinach, and goat cheese roll-ups
4. A handful of pumpkin seeds
5. Frozen grapes
6. Cucumber slices marinated in vinegar
7. Ants on a Log (celery sticks with natural peanut butter and raisins)
8. A pear and white Cheddar cheese
9. Sliced avocado and tomatoes
10. Salt and Pepper Kale Chips*
11. Spiced Pecan-Almond Granola with Dried Fruit*
12. Beet Chips with Creamy Goat Cheese Dip*

Recipe included in recipe section

Week Three Pantry

OILS AND VINEGARS

- Oil, avocado
- Oil, coconut
- Oil, extra-virgin olive
- Vinegar, apple cider
- Vinegar, balsamic
- Vinegar, white wine

HERBS AND SPICES

- Chili powder
- Cinnamon, ground
- Cumin, ground
- Garlic powder
- Italian seasoning
- Nutmeg, ground
- Oregano, dried
- Paprika, smoked
- Pepper, black
- Salt

SWEETENERS

- Cane juice, evaporated
- Coconut sugar
- Honey
- Maple syrup, pure

FLOURS AND GRAINS

- Almond flour
- Barley
- Bread crumbs, 100% whole-wheat panko
- Flour, 100% whole-wheat pastry
- Oats, rolled
- Pasta, 100% whole-grain elbow
- Pasta, 100% whole-grain fusilli
- Rice, brown, short-grain

CONDIMENTS

- Mustard, Dijon
- Tamari or coconut aminos

DRIED FRUIT

- Apples, dried, unsweetened
- Raisins, unsweetened

NUTS AND SEEDS

- Pecans, chopped
- Pine nuts
- Walnuts

OTHER

- Arrowroot powder
- Artichoke hearts, jarred
- Baking powder
- Baking soda
- Chocolate, 70% bittersweet
- Coconut, unsweetened shredded
- Cream of tartar
- Peppermint extract, pure
- Peppers, chipotle in adobo sauce
- Peppers, red, roasted
- Tomatoes, sun-dried
- Vanilla extract, pure

Week Three Shopping List

VEGETABLES

- Avocado (4)
- Baby spinach, fresh (three 11-ounce clamshells)
- Beets (1 pound)
- Bell pepper, red (1)
- Carrots (2)
- Cucumber (2)
- Jalapeño pepper (1)
- Kale (2 pounds)
- Lettuce, mixed baby (10 ounces)
- Onions (5)
- Pears (2)
- Peas and carrots, frozen mix (one 16-ounce bag)
- Potatoes, new (1 pound)
- Tomatoes (6)
- Zucchini (2)

HERBS AND SPICES

- Basil (2 bunches)
- Cilantro (1 bunch)
- Garlic cloves (2 heads)
- Ginger (one 3-inch piece)

GRAINS

- Pitas, 100% whole-wheat (2)
- Tortillas, sprouted-grain or 100% whole-wheat (eight 6-inch)

FRUIT

- Bananas (7)
- Lemons (3)
- Lime (1)
- Orange (1)
- Pears (4)
- Strawberries (1 quart)

MEAT AND FISH

- Beef, ground round (1½ pounds)
- Chicken breasts, boneless, skinless (1½ pounds)
- Flounder fillets (4)
- Turkey, deli-roasted, sliced (1 pound)
- Turkey sausage, Italian (8 ounces)

EGGS AND DAIRY

- Butter (1 stick)
- Cheese, Cheddar, white (8 ounces)
- Cheese, feta (4 ounces)
- Cheese, goat (4 ounces)
- Cheese, Parmesan (6 ounces)
- Eggs (32)
- Milk (1 quart)
- Yogurt, Greek, plain (2 small containers)

OTHER

- Beans, black (one 15-ounce can)
- Beans, kidney (one 15-ounce can)
- Bread, sprouted-grain, frozen (2 loaves)
- Broth, beef, reduced-sodium (one 14-ounce can)
- Broth, chicken, reduced-sodium (two 32-ounce cartons)
- Broth, vegetable, reduced-sodium (one 32-ounce carton)
- Chickpeas (one 15-ounce can)
- Coconut milk (two 13.5-ounce cans)
- Lentils, brown (8 ounces)
- Tomato paste (two 12-ounce cans)
- Tomatoes, whole in puree (three 28-ounce cans)
- Tuna, albacore in water (two 5-ounce cans)

Prep Ahead

On the weekend or when you find free time, make these recipes ahead of time to help you out during the following week:

- **Fresh Salsa** (page 297)
- **Homemade Mayonnaise** (page 288)
- **Spiced Pecan-Almond Granola with Dried Fruit** (page 138)

Week Four

Congratulations! You've made it to the last week of the meal plan! Over the past few weeks, you've learned the necessary concepts and tools for your new lifestyle. Keep these clean eating principles in mind this week:

1 **On-the-Go:** Don't forget to pack snacks to take with you to work to have on hand during the day. And always eat breakfast. Smoothies can be poured into a travel mug or sports bottle if your morning doesn't allow the time to sit down. Muffins and banana bread are other breakfasts that can quickly be divided and put in sealed containers for easy transport.

2 **Looking Ahead:** This week you may begin looking ahead to a week outside of the meal plan. You always have the option of repeating this meal plan, but if you'd like to try cooking on your own, don't be overwhelmed. Remember to plan ahead and make a grocery list. When selecting recipes, you may want to choose some with similar items to help you save at the store.

Week Four Menu at a Glance

DAY ONE

Breakfast Banana Nut Bread (from Week Three)
Lunch Corn and Potato Chowder
Dinner Loaded Pinto Bean Nachos (uses Fresh Salsa from Week Three)
Dessert Apple Crumble

DAY TWO

Breakfast Peach-Oat Smoothie
Lunch Black Bean Soup (double to use on Day Six; uses Fresh Salsa from Week Three)

Dinner Skillet-Barbecued Chicken with Mustard Green Bean–Potato Salad (uses Mustard-Thyme Vinaigrette from Week Three and Homemade Mayonnaise from Week Three)
Dessert Frozen Blueberry-Granola Bars

DAY THREE

Breakfast Vegetable Omelet with Goat Cheese
Lunch Almond Butter–Apple Sandwiches
Dinner Grilled Flank Steak with Cucumber, Tomato, and Corn Relish
Dessert Fudgy Chocolate Chunk–Pecan Brownies

DAY FOUR

Breakfast Green Tea, Cucumber, and Mint Smoothie and Toast with Creamy Natural Peanut Butter
Lunch Southwestern Salad with Shrimp and Black Beans (uses Cilantro-Lime Vinaigrette from Week Two)
Dinner Pork and Peach Skewers with Grilled Asparagus
Dessert Quick Vanilla Pudding

DAY FIVE

Breakfast Yogurt-Berry Parfait (uses Spiced Pecan-Almond Granola with Dried Fruit from Week Three)
Lunch Chicken-Pesto BLT (uses Basil Pesto from Week Two and chicken from Day Two)
Dinner Sweet Chili-Tofu and Sugar Snap Stir-Fry
Dessert Dark Cherry, Pistachio, Coconut, and Bittersweet Chocolate Bark

DAY SIX

Breakfast Pumpkin-Pecan Breakfast Cookies
Lunch Black Bean Soup
Dinner Maple-Sage Pork Tenderloin with Sautéed Mushroom Farro
Dessert Frozen Blueberry-Granola Bars (uses granola from Day Two)

DAY SEVEN

Breakfast Chocolate–Peanut Butter Smoothie
Lunch Creamy Asparagus Soup
Dinner Coconut Shrimp with Sesame Green Beans (uses Honey-Mustard Dipping Sauce)
Dessert Fudgy Chocolate Chunk–Pecan Brownies

Weekly Snacks
Choose one or two each day.
1. Apple slices with Creamy Natural Peanut Butter*
2. Sliced cucumbers with Greek yogurt seasoned with curry powder
3. One cup of sliced peaches and blueberries tossed with mint, honey, and lemon juice
4. A handful of pecans
5. A hard-boiled egg
6. Sliced tomatoes with crumbled goat cheese and fresh basil
7. Steamed edamame
8. Fresh pineapple chunks
9. One banana
10. Slow Cooker Applesauce*
11. Garlic-Herb Popcorn*
12. Cranberry, Cinnamon, and Oat Bars*

Recipe included in recipe section

Week Four Pantry

OILS AND VINEGARS

- Oil, avocado
- Oil, coconut
- Oil, extra-virgin olive
- Vinegar, apple cider

HERBS AND SPICES

- Allspice
- Chili powder
- Cinnamon, ground
- Cumin, ground
- Curry powder
- Italian seasoning
- Nutmeg, ground
- Pepper, black
- Salt
- Thyme, dried

SWEETENERS

- Cane juice, evaporated
- Coconut sugar
- Honey
- Maple syrup, pure

FLOURS AND GRAINS

- Farro
- Flour, 100% whole-wheat pastry
- Oats, rolled

CONDIMENTS

- Hot sauce, sambal oelek chili
- Mustard, Dijon
- Mustard, grainy Dijon
- Tamari or coconut aminos

DRIED FRUIT AND NUT BUTTERS

- Almond butter, all-natural
- Apricots, dried
- Cherries, dried unsweetened
- Cranberries, dried unsweetened

NUTS

- Almonds, whole
- Peanuts, dry-roasted
- Pecans, chopped
- Pistachios, unsalted, shelled

OTHER

- Almond extract
- Arrowroot powder
- Baking powder
- Chocolate, 70% bittersweet
- Cocoa powder, unsweetened
- Coconut, unsweetened shredded
- Peppers, red, roasted, jarred
- Pumpkin, canned unsweetened
- Tea, green
- Vanilla extract, pure

Week Four Shopping List

VEGETABLES

- Asparagus (3½ pounds)
- Avocados (2)
- Baby spinach, fresh (one 10-ounce bag)
- Corn (5 ears)
- Cucumbers (2)
- Lettuce, romaine (2 heads)
- Mushrooms (1½ pounds)
- Jalapeño pepper (1)
- Onions (3)
- Potatoes, new (2 pounds)
- Tomatoes (9)
- Vegetables, stir-fry mix, without sauce, frozen (one 12-ounce bag)

HERBS AND SPICES

- Basil (1 bunch)
- Cilantro (1 bunch)
- Mint (1 bunch)
- Garlic cloves (2 heads)
- Ginger (2-inch piece)

GRAINS

- Bread, sprouted-grain, frozen (1 loaf)
- Noodles, brown rice (one 8-ounce package)
- Tortillas, sprouted-grain or 100% whole-wheat (eight 6-inch)

FRUIT

- Apples (6)
- Banana (1)
- Blueberries (1 quart)
- Lemon (1)
- Limes (2)
- Peaches (3)
- Peaches, slices, frozen (one 16-ounce bag)
- Strawberries (1 pint)

MEAT AND FISH

- Bacon, uncured (6 slices)
- Chicken breasts, boneless, skinless (6)
- Pork tenderloin (3 pounds)
- Shrimp, large, deveined and peeled (2½ pounds)
- Steak, flank (2 pounds)

EGGS AND DAIRY

- Butter (2 sticks)
- Cheese, feta (6 ounces)
- Cheese, goat (2 ounces)
- Eggs (1 dozen)
- Milk (1 quart)
- Sour cream (8 ounces)
- Tofu, firm
  (one 12-ounce container)
- Yogurt, Greek, plain
  (40 ounces)

OTHER

- Beans, black (four
  15-ounce cans)
- Beans, pinto (two
  15-ounce cans)
- Broth, vegetable,
  reduced-sodium
  (three 14.5-ounce cans)
- Chia seeds (⅛ pound)
- Coconut milk
  (one 13.5-ounce can)
- Green beans
  (one 24-ounce package)
- Pineapple juice,
  unsweetened (small carton)

Prep Ahead

On the weekend or when you find free time, make these recipes ahead of time to help you out during the following week:

- **Black Bean Soup** (page 116)

- **Pumpkin-Pecan Breakfast Cookies** (page 95)

- **Slow Cooker Applesauce** (page 150)

II

Eating Clean

4

Smoothies

Green Tea, Cucumber, and Mint Smoothie

Green tea, ginger, cucumber, and mint are an excellent combination for promoting good digestion. This low-calorie smoothie will rehydrate you any time of day. Because it is low in calories, serve it with a piece of toast spread with nut butter for a balanced breakfast or lunch.

Make-Ahead Tip: Brew and chill the green tea the day before, so it's ready to go in the morning on your way out the door.

1½ cups strong, brewed green tea, chilled

1 tablespoon fresh lemon juice

1½ teaspoons grated peeled fresh ginger

½ small cucumber, peeled and coarsely chopped

2 tablespoons fresh mint leaves

½ cup ice

Combine the tea, lemon juice, ginger, cucumber, mint leaves, and ice in a blender. Cover and blend to the desired smoothness. Serve immediately.

Serves 2. Prep time: 15 minutes.

Per serving: Calories: 21   Fat: 0.3g   Saturated Fat: 0g   Protein: 0.8g
Carbohydrates: 4.3g   Fiber: 1.0g

Almond, Cherry, and Vanilla Smoothie

Vegan
Gluten-Free

Cherries are a good source of dietary fiber and you get an extra boost from flaxseed. This recipe uses unsweetened almond milk, a perfect choice for those sensitive to dairy. If you prefer, you can use regular cow's milk in place of the almond milk.

Time-Saving Tip: A cherry pitter makes easy work of removing the pits from the cherries in the recipe. If you don't have a cherry pitter or don't want to make the investment, a pastry tip or chopstick works well, too.

1½ cups unsweetened
    almond milk
2 cups pitted cherries
¼ teaspoon pure vanilla
    extract

⅛ teaspoon almond extract
1½ teaspoons flaxseed
½ cup ice

Combine the almond milk, cherries, vanilla, almond extract, flaxseed, and ice in a blender. Cover and blend to the desired smoothness. Serve immediately.

Serves 2. Prep time: 10 minutes.

. . . .

Per serving: Calories: 132   Fat: 2.8g   Saturated Fat: 0g   Protein: 3.1g
Carbohydrates: 24.1g   Fiber: 4.2g

Vegan
Gluten-Free

Avocado-Lime Smoothie

Avocado might seem an odd ingredient for a smoothie, but give it a try. You'll find it is delightfully creamy and has a subtle flavor. Lime is really the featured flavor in this drink. Together lime and avocado have lots of heart-healthy monounsaturated fats and vitamin C.

Ingredient Tip: Because you are using the lime zest in this recipe, buy organic limes if they are available.

1 avocado

1½ cups unsweetened
    almond milk

1½ teaspoons lime juice

¼ teaspoon lime zest

1½ teaspoons honey

¼ teaspoon pure
    vanilla extract

Combine the avocado, almond milk, lime juice and zest, honey, and vanilla in a blender. Cover and blend to the desired smoothness. Serve immediately.

Serves 2. Prep time: 5 minutes.

. . . .

Per serving: Calories: 248   Fat: 21.5g   Saturated Fat: 4.1g   Protein: 2.7g
Carbohydrates: 14.8g   Fiber: 7.6g

Banana, Strawberry, and Walnut Smoothie

Vegan
Gluten-Free

Walnuts are a delicious inclusion in this tasty banana and strawberry smoothie. They are a good source of heart-healthy vitamin E, provide many antioxidant benefits, and also offer healthy omega-3 fatty acids.

Ingredient Tip: Are strawberries not in season? No problem. Opt for frozen sliced strawberries instead and increase the amount of fresh orange juice to reach the right thickness. You can also leave the banana unfrozen.

1 banana, peeled and frozen

1½ cups fresh strawberries, halved

¼ cup freshly squeezed orange juice (about 1 orange)

2 tablespoons chopped walnuts

Combine the banana, strawberries, orange juice, and walnuts in a blender. Cover and blend to the desired smoothness. Serve immediately.

Serves 2. Prep time: 5 minutes.

. . . .

Per serving: Calories: 149   Fat: 5g   Saturated Fat: 0g   Protein: 3.4g
Carbohydrates: 25.7g   Fiber: 4.5g

Tropical Smoothie

Get your day started with a taste from the tropics. Naturally sweet pineapple is blended with tangy ginger and a hint of orange in this yummy smoothie. For an especially kid-friendly version, add some fresh berries.

Ingredient Tip: Looking for an easy way to prepare ginger? Use the sides of a spoon to peel the skin. Then, use the small holes on a box grater to grate it. Ginger also freezes well in an ice cube tray.

1½ cups frozen
   pineapple chunks

1½ tablespoon peeled, grated
   fresh ginger

½ cup freshly squeezed orange
   juice (about 2 oranges)

¼ cup milk

Combine the pineapple, ginger, orange juice, and milk in a blender. Cover and blend to the desired smoothness. Serve immediately.

Serves 2. Prep time: 5 minutes.

Per serving: Calories: 124   Fat: 0.8g   Saturated Fat: 0g   Protein: 1.4g
Carbohydrates: 28.2g   Fiber: 3.1g

Peach-Oat Smoothie

Old-fashioned oats are the secret ingredient in this sweet smoothie. They provide thickness and fiber, and you probably won't even notice that they're in there. In addition to heart-healthy oats, chia seeds are added for even more fiber and healthy omega-3s. As tiny as chia seeds are, they are a whole food and an easily absorbed source of omega-3 fatty acids, carbohydrates, protein, fiber, anti-oxidants, and calcium.

Ingredient Variations: This fruity smoothie highlights sweet peaches but feel free to use other frozen fruits. Mixed berries, strawberries, and bananas are all good options.

½ cup milk

½ cup plain Greek yogurt

2½ tablespoons uncooked
  old-fashioned oats

1½ tablespoons honey

1 tablespoon chia seeds

1½ cups frozen sliced peaches

1. Combine the milk, yogurt, oats, honey, and chia seeds in a blender. Let it stand for 5 minutes or until the chia seeds soften.
2. Add the peaches. Cover and blend to the desired smoothness. Serve immediately.

Serves 2. Prep time: 5 minutes.

. . . .

Per serving: Calories: 223   Fat: 5.8g   Saturated Fat: 2.2g   Protein: 9.1g
Carbohydrates: 35.3g   Fiber: 4.7g

Mango Lassi Smoothie

A lassi is a popular Indian drink, and this bright, refreshing mango version is a wonderful way to start your day. Exotic cardamom and tart yogurt combine perfectly with the sweet tropical flavor of mango.

Ingredient Tip: Mango is the star of this smoothie, and it makes a great addition to many varieties of smoothie. Add frozen mango chunks to the blender with spinach, a few squeezes of lime, a frozen banana, and milk or water for a nutritious green smoothie.

1½ cups frozen chopped mango

1 cup plain Greek yogurt

2 tablespoons milk

¼ teaspoon ground cardamom

1 tablespoon honey

Combine the mango, yogurt, milk, cardamom, and honey in a blender. Cover and blend to the desired smoothness. Serve immediately.

Serves 2. Prep time: 5 minutes.

Per serving: Calories: 205   Fat: 4.8g   Saturated Fat: 3.2g   Protein: 11.6g
Carbohydrates: 33.1g   Fiber: 2.1g

Ginger-Coconut Smoothie

This is one decadently rich and satisfying smoothie. Ginger is known for its healing properties and together with coconut and banana, it gives the smoothie a tropical taste. Because the fat content is on the high side, be mindful of what you eat throughout the rest of the day. If you prefer a lighter version, you can always substitute milk or almond milk for some of the coconut milk.

Ingredient Tip: Coconut milk tends to separate in the can, so shake it to mix it up before you use it.

½ cup unsweetened
    flaked coconut

1 banana, peeled and frozen

1 cup coconut milk

1½ teaspoons honey

¼ cup ice

1½ teaspoons grated
    fresh ginger

Combine the flaked coconut, banana, coconut milk, honey, ice, and ginger in a blender. Cover and blend to the desired smoothness. Serve immediately.

Serves 2. Prep time: 10 minutes.

Per serving: Calories: 364   Fat: 29.6g   Saturated Fat: 26.2g   Protein: 3.6g
Carbohydrates: 27.1g   Fiber: 5.8g

Chocolate–Peanut Butter Smoothie

Vegetarian
Gluten-Free

Who says you can't have dessert for breakfast? This indulgent smoothie is packed with protein, while satisfying every peanut butter and chocolate lover's palate. It uses homemade peanut butter, which you'll find super easy to make.

Time-Saving Tip: If you don't have time to make the peanut butter, you can buy all-natural peanut butter at the store. Just be sure to check the label to make sure that all you're getting is ground peanuts.

¼ cup Creamy Natural Peanut
    Butter (page 306)
3 tablespoons unsweetened
    cocoa powder

1½ cups milk
½ cup plain Greek yogurt
1 banana, peeled and frozen
1 tablespoon honey

Combine the peanut butter, cocoa powder, milk, yogurt, banana, and honey in a blender. Cover and blend to the desired smoothness. Serve immediately.

Serves 4. Prep time: 20 minutes.

Per serving: Calories: 346 Fat: 16.7g Saturated Fat: 6.7g Protein: 19.5g
Carbohydrates: 34g Fiber: 3.2g

Triple-Berry Smoothie

Vegetarian
Gluten-Free

Blueberries and strawberries are considered superfoods since both contain antioxidants that help ward off disease. A superfood hidden in this smoothie that you won't even taste is spinach. Spinach is one of the world's healthiest foods. It contains many vitamins and minerals but also phytonutrients such as carotenoids (beta-carotene, lutein, and zeaxanthin) and flavonoids that promote good health.

Ingredient Tip: Take advantage of grocery store sales or in-season produce at the farmers' market. Buy extra fresh blueberries, strawberries, and blackberries and store them in zip-top plastic freezer bags for times when the produce is not in season.

1 cup frozen mixed berries
  (blueberries, strawberries,
  and blackberries)
²/₃ cup fresh baby spinach

1 cup plain Greek yogurt
1 tablespoon honey
½ cup freshly squeezed orange
  juice (about 2 oranges)

Place the berries, spinach, yogurt, and honey in a blender and pour the orange juice over the top. Cover and blend to the desired smoothness. Serve immediately.

Serves 2. Prep time: 5 minutes.

. . . .

Per serving: Calories: 151.9   Fat: 0.1g   Saturated Fat: 0g   Protein: 11.2g
Carbohydrates: 28.6g   Fiber: 3.1g

5

Breakfast

Yogurt-Berry Parfait

Between layers of naturally sweet fruit, sprinkle in some homemade granola for a healthy crunch. The recipe calls for spicy-sweet granola, but any clean granola will do. This parfait travels easily and makes for the perfect at-work breakfast or afternoon snack.

Ingredient Variations: You can use any leftover fruit you may have in your refrigerator in place of strawberries and blueberries. And if time is tight, you can always substitute store-bought granola for homemade. Just be sure to read the label to confirm that there's no added refined sugar.

1 cup plain Greek yogurt

1 tablespoon honey

8 tablespoons Spiced Pecan-
    Almond Granola with Dried
    Fruit (page 138)

½ cup sliced strawberries

½ cup blueberries

1. In a medium bowl, stir together the yogurt and honey.
2. Spoon ¼ cup of the yogurt mixture into each of the two serving bowls.
3. On top of the yogurt, sprinkle 2 tablespoons of the granola and top with ¼ cup of the strawberries. Repeat the yogurt layer and top with ¼ cup of the blueberries.
4. Serve right away, or refrigerate for up to 1 hour.

Serves 2. Prep time: 10 minutes.

Per serving: Calories: 235   Fat: 19.9g   Saturated Fat: 5.5g   Protein: 19.3g
Carbohydrates: 53.4g   Fiber: 7g

Slow Cooker Overnight Oatmeal with Fresh Cherries and Maple Syrup

Steel-cut oats are a little bit more crunchy than traditional rolled oats. They're also slightly lower in calories and pack a higher punch of fiber. The tart-sweet cherries and sweet maple syrup complete this delicious, healthy breakfast dish.

Cooking Tip: Don't have a slow cooker? This oatmeal can be made on the stove top, too. Follow the instructions on the package for cooking times.

Coconut oil, for greasing

1 (13.5-ounce) can coconut milk

3¼ cups water

1 cup steel-cut oats

½ cup pure maple syrup

¼ teaspoon salt

1 teaspoon pure vanilla extract

½ teaspoon ground cinnamon

2 cups fresh cherries, pitted and halved

1. Coat a 3- to 4-quart slow cooker with coconut oil. Combine the coconut milk, water, oats, maple syrup, and salt in the slow cooker. Cover and cook on low for 7 hours or until the oats are tender and the mixture is creamy. Stir in the vanilla and cinnamon.
2. Divide the oatmeal among serving bowls, top each bowl with the fresh cherries, and serve.

Serves 4. Prep time: 10 minutes. Cooking time: 7 hours.
Total time: 7 hours, 10 minutes.

. . . .
Per serving: Calories: 529   Fat: 25.4g   Saturated Fat: 20.7g   Protein: 9.2g
Carbohydrates: 70.1g   Fiber: 7.8g

Streusel-Topped Blueberry Muffins

These tender treats studded with juicy blueberries are sure to be a hit. The crumbly streusel topping adds a crunch with the cinnamon-spiced almonds. These can also be made in advance and stored in an airtight container for an on-the-go snack or meal. If you're making the muffins while following the meal plan, freeze them in a layer of plastic wrap and then cover with foil. Defrost in the plastic wrap for 3 to 4 hours at room temperature.

Cooking Tip: For the fluffiest, most tender muffin, be careful not to over-stir the batter, which can make the muffins tough. Instead, stir the wet ingredients into the dry ingredients gently, just until the dry ingredients are moistened.

For the topping:

3 tablespoons 100% whole-wheat pastry flour

3 tablespoons evaporated cane juice

¼ cup finely chopped dry-roasted almonds

½ teaspoon ground cinnamon

2 tablespoons butter, melted

For the muffins:

2 cups 100% whole-wheat pastry flour

1 teaspoon baking soda

½ teaspoon salt

2 cups fresh blueberries

1 cup Slow Cooker Applesauce (page 150) or store-bought unsweetened applesauce

¼ cup evaporated cane juice

1 teaspoon pure vanilla extract

1 egg, beaten

2 tablespoons butter, melted

To make the topping:

In a small bowl, stir together the flour, cane juice, almonds, cinnamon, and butter. Stir with a fork until moistened.

continued ▶

To make the muffins:

1. Preheat the oven to 325°F.
2. Line 12 cups of a muffin tin with paper liners.
3. In a large bowl, whisk together the flour, baking soda, and salt; add the blueberries, tossing gently to coat.
4. In a separate bowl, whisk together the applesauce, cane juice, vanilla extract, egg, and butter. Add the applesauce mixture to the flour mixture and stir until just moistened.
5. Spoon the mixture into the paper liners. Crumble the topping evenly over the muffins.
6. Bake for 23 to 25 minutes or until the topping is lightly browned and a toothpick inserted in the center comes out clean. Remove the muffins from the oven and let them cool in the pan for 10 minutes.
7. Serve warm or remove to a cooling rack and cool completely.

Makes 12 muffins. Prep time: 15 minutes. Cooking time: 25 minutes.
Total time: 40 minutes (plus 10 minutes to cool).
. . . .

Per serving: Calories: 144   Fat: 5.6g   Saturated Fat: 2.6g   Protein: 3.2g
Carbohydrates: 19.9g   Fiber: 2.8g

Pumpkin-Pecan Breakfast Cookies

Vegan
Gluten-Free

Cookies for breakfast? Absolutely! These chewy treats are packed with a satisfying amount of sweetness to get your day started. The old-fashioned rolled oats are a great cholesterol reducer. Along with fiber-rich pecans, you will feel full all morning long.

Ingredient Tip: Be sure to buy unsweetened canned pumpkin instead of pumpkin pie filling. They are usually on the market shelf together, and the pie filling is loaded with extra sugar.

1½ cups uncooked old-fashioned rolled oats

⅔ cup unsweetened canned pumpkin

1 cup Slow Cooker Applesauce (page 150) or store-bought unsweetened applesauce

⅓ cup chopped pecans, toasted

¼ cup dried unsweetened cranberries

1 teaspoon pure vanilla extract

1. Preheat the oven to 350°F.
2. Line a rimmed baking sheet with parchment paper.
3. In a large bowl, stir together the oats, canned pumpkin, apple-sauce, pecans, cranberries, and vanilla; let the mixture stand for 10 minutes. Drop the dough in 12 rounds onto the baking sheet, spacing them 2 inches apart. Flatten the dough mounds.
4. Bake for 20 to 25 minutes or until the cookies are golden brown. Remove the pan from the oven and let the cookies stand for 5 minutes on the baking sheet before removing them to cooling racks to cool completely.
5. Serve.

Makes 12 cookies. Prep time: 10 minutes. Cooking time: 20 minutes. Total time: 30 minutes (plus 5 minutes to cool).

Per serving: Calories: 81   Fat: 3.2g
Saturated Fat: 0g   Protein: 1.8g   Carbohydrates: 10.8g   Fiber: 1.9g

Nutty Whole-Grain Waffles

Toasted pecans add a surprising crunch and some extra protein to these hearty waffles. For a delicious alternative, try serving Warm Berry Sauce (page 308) on these waffles instead of the maple syrup.

Double It: The next time you make these waffles, why not double the recipe and keep the prepared waffles on hand. They freeze well and can be thawed by popping them in the toaster.

2 eggs

1¾ cups unsweetened
   almond milk

¼ cup butter, melted, plus
   1 tablespoon

2 tablespoons honey

½ teaspoon ground cinnamon

¼ teaspoon baking soda

1½ cups 100% whole-wheat
   pastry flour

2 teaspoons baking powder

Pinch salt

½ cup chopped pecans,
   toasted

¾ cup pure maple syrup

1. Preheat a waffle iron.
2. In a large bowl, whisk together the eggs, almond milk, ¼ cup of butter, honey, cinnamon, and baking soda.
3. In a separate bowl, stir together the flour, baking powder, salt, and pecans. Add the dry ingredients to the egg mixture, whisking until combined.
4. Brush the hot waffle iron with the remaining 1 tablespoon of butter. Ladle batter onto the waffle iron. Cook for 3 to 4 minutes or according to the manufacturer's instructions. Repeat with the remaining batter.
5. Serve warm. Top each serving with maple syrup.

Serves 4. Prep time: 10 minutes. Cooking time: 5 minutes (per batch). Total time: 15 minutes.

. . . .

Per serving: Calories: 488   Fat: 23.6g   Saturated Fat: 8.7g   Protein: 7.5g
Carbohydrates: 66.8g   Fiber: 3.3g

Baked Banana French Toast

Say hello to French toast that is good for you! Since bread is the star here, use a good quality sprouted-grain or whole-wheat bread. Coconut is used for the oil and sugar, making it a clean eating choice. If you want to make it ahead, prepare the casserole through step three, cover, and refrigerate overnight. The next morning, let it stand at room temperature for 30 minutes before baking. Yum!

Double It: Feed a crowd with this family favorite. Double all of the ingredients and bake it in a 13-by-9-inch baking dish.

Coconut oil, for greasing

6 slices frozen sprouted-grain bread, thawed and halved

2 bananas, sliced

3 eggs

1½ cups milk

½ teaspoon ground cinnamon

¼ teaspoon freshly grated nutmeg

1 teaspoon pure vanilla extract

¼ cup coconut sugar

Pure maple syrup, for serving

1. Preheat the oven to 350°F.
2. Grease an 8-inch-square baking dish with coconut oil.
3. Arrange the bread slices in the prepared dish, cutting the bread in half, if needed. Place sliced bananas in between bread slices.
4. In a large bowl, whisk together the eggs, milk, cinnamon, nutmeg, vanilla, and sugar. Slowly pour the mixture over the bread slices. Press the bread to allow it to soak up the egg mixture.
5. Bake for 45 to 50 minutes, or until the eggs are set and the casserole is golden brown.
6. Cool slightly. Cut the casserole into servings and drizzle with the maple syrup.

Serves 4. Prep time: 10 minutes. Cooking time: 45 minutes. Total time: 55 minutes.

Per serving: Calories: 315   Fat: 5.3g   Saturated Fat: 2.2g   Protein: 13.8g
Carbohydrates: 53.1g   Fiber: 6.4g

Banana Nut Bread

Vegetarian
Dairy-Free

Old-fashioned banana nut bread meets clean eating and the result is the perfect amount of sweetness to satisfy your craving. It's also great to make ahead and keep in the refrigerator for a few days, or the freezer for a longer amount of time. Banana bread freezes very well. If this dessert is part of your eating plan you may want to wrap individual slices in foil to defrost whenever the sweet urge hits.

Ingredient Tip: Measure mashed bananas with this easy trick. Place very-ripe bananas in a zip-top plastic bag. Seal and squish the bananas with your fingers until they're mashed. Snip a corner off the bag and squeeze the bananas into a measuring cup.

1¼ cups 100% whole-wheat
    pastry flour
1 teaspoon baking soda
¼ teaspoon salt
2 eggs
1 teaspoon pure vanilla extract
½ cup coconut oil, plus
    additional for greasing pan

¼ cup evaporated cane juice
1½ cups mashed bananas
    (about 3 ripe)
½ cup chopped walnuts,
    toasted

1. Preheat the oven to 350°F.
2. Coat a 9-by-5-inch loaf pan with coconut oil.
3. In a medium bowl, whisk together the flour, baking soda, and salt.
4. In a separate medium bowl, whisk together the eggs, vanilla, oil, cane juice, and bananas. Add the wet ingredients to the flour. Stir until combined. Fold in the nuts.
5. Pour the batter into the prepared pan. Bake for 45 to 50 minutes, or until a toothpick inserted in the center comes out clean. Cool the bread in the pan for 5 minutes. Remove the bread from the pan to a cooling rack and allow it to cool completely.
6. Slice and serve.

Serves 8. Prep time: 10 minutes. Cooking time: 45 minutes. Total time: 55 minutes.

Per serving: Calories: 254 Fat: 19.5g Saturated Fat: 12.4g Protein: 4.9g
Carbohydrates: 17.4g Fiber: 2.5g

Eggs Baked in Toast Cups

The humble egg is highlighted in a new way in these crunchy toast cups covered by a sprinkling of melted cheese. Sprouted-grain bread acts as the perfect holder and complements both a runny or firm egg yolk to perfection. With additional flavors of sweet tomato and basil, it'll be hard to eat just one. These are perfect grab-and-go items.

Ingredient Variations: This breakfast dish is sure to be a favorite, especially with kids, and can be adjusted in many ways for a different taste. Try other chopped vegetables, like onions, and alternative types of cheese and herbs. The options are endless!

3 tablespoons coconut oil

4 slices frozen sprouted-grain bread, thawed

4 eggs

½ cup chopped tomato

½ cup shredded white Cheddar cheese

2 tablespoons chopped fresh basil

½ teaspoon salt

½ teaspoon freshly ground black pepper

1. Preheat the oven to 375°F.
2. Brush 4 cups of a muffin tin with 1 tablespoon of coconut oil.
3. Remove the crusts from the bread. With a rolling pin, press the bread to ¼ inch thickness.
4. Brush the bread with the remaining 2 tablespoons of coconut oil, and press the bread into the prepared muffin tin to create a bowl.
5. Carefully crack an egg into each cup. Top each egg evenly with tomato, cheese, basil, salt, and pepper. Bake for 20 minutes or until the eggs are set.
6. Use the tip of a knife to loosen the cups from the edges of the pan. Serve.

Serves 4. Prep time: 10 minutes. Cooking time: 20 minutes. Total time: 30 minutes.

Per serving: Calories: 263   Fat: 16g   Saturated Fat: 10.2g   Protein: 13.3g
Carbohydrates: 16.5g   Fiber: 3.3g

Vegetable Omelet with Goat Cheese

Goat cheese adds a healthy tanginess to this vegetable-filled omelet. Try experimenting with your favorite combinations. For a country omelet, serve with hash browns, onions, and peppers, or use any other vegetables you may have on hand.

Ingredient Tip: Did you know that goat cheese is often digestible for people with lactose intolerance? The reason has to do with the molecular difference between cow's milk and goat's milk.

1 tablespoon avocado oil

3 cups chopped fresh mushrooms

2 cups chopped fresh baby spinach

½ cup chopped roasted red peppers

½ cup chopped onion

1 teaspoon Italian seasoning

½ teaspoon salt

½ teaspoon freshly ground black pepper

5 eggs, lightly beaten

2 ounces crumbled goat cheese

1. Heat the oil in a large nonstick skillet over medium-high heat; add mushrooms, spinach, red peppers, onion, Italian seasoning, and ¼ teaspoon each of salt and pepper.
2. Sauté the mixture for 5 minutes or until tender. Remove the mixture from the skillet and keep warm.
3. Whisk together the eggs and remaining ¼ teaspoon each of salt and pepper. Add to skillet. Tilt the pan to coat evenly with the egg.
4. Cook for 1 minute or until the egg begins to set. Use a spatula to lift edges and allow uncooked egg to flow underneath. Cook for 2 more minutes or until the egg is almost set.
5. Sprinkle goat cheese on top of the egg; spread the vegetable mixture over the goat cheese. Fold the omelet in half and cook for 1 more minute or until cheese softens and egg is cooked through.
6. Slide the omelet onto a plate and cut it in half before serving.

Serves 2. Prep time: 15 minutes. Cooking time: 10 minutes. Total time: 25 minutes.

. . . .

Per serving: Calories: 357   Fat: 23.1g   Saturated Fat: 10.7g   Protein: 27.4g
Carbohydrates: 12.5g   Fiber: 3.3g

Eggs Poached in Spiced Tomato Sauce

The marinara sauce gives this egg dish an extra kick. Poaching the eggs right in the sauce adds tons of extra flavor. Garnish with chopped flat-leaf parsley, if desired, and serve on sprouted-grain bread for a delicious, energy-rich, satisfying meal to start the day.

Make-Ahead Tip: The marinara sauce can be made days in advance and stored in an airtight container in the refrigerator.

2 tablespoons avocado oil

½ cup chopped onion

½ teaspoon ground cumin

2 cups Homemade Marinara Sauce (page 294)

4 eggs

¼ teaspoon salt

¼ teaspoon freshly ground black pepper

4 slices frozen sprouted-grain bread, thawed and toasted

1. In a large deep skillet, heat the oil over medium heat. Add the onion and cumin. Cook, stirring occasionally, for 5 minutes, or until the onion is tender.
2. Add the marinara sauce. Cook for 5 minutes until gently bubbling.
3. Crack the eggs into the sauce. Sprinkle the dish with salt and pepper. Cover and cook for 5 to 8 minutes or until desired doneness.
4. Spoon 1 egg and some of the sauce onto each piece of toast. Serve.

Serves 4. Prep time: 10 minutes. Cooking time: 15 minutes. Total time: 25 minutes.

. . . .

Per serving: Calories: 268 Fat: 8.7g Saturated Fat: 2.4g Protein: 12g
Carbohydrates: 34.5g Fiber: 6.9g

Spinach–Red Pepper Frittata with Feta

This colorful frittata is as delicious as it is beautiful. The roasted red peppers are a handy clean eating convenience item that packs a punch of flavor. Be sure to pat them dry with paper towels before adding them to the pan.

Perfect Pair: This frittata is delicious served for lunch or dinner. Pair it with a green salad drizzled with the Honey-Balsamic Vinaigrette (page 301) for an easy meal.

2 tablespoons coconut oil

3 cups firmly packed fresh
   baby spinach

1 garlic clove, minced

8 eggs

½ teaspoon salt

½ teaspoon freshly ground
   black pepper

¼ teaspoon freshly
   ground nutmeg

2 jarred roasted red peppers,
   thinly sliced

½ cup crumbled feta cheese

2 tablespoons chopped
   fresh basil

1. In a 10-inch nonstick skillet, heat the coconut oil over medium heat. Add the spinach and garlic and cook, stirring occasionally, for 2 minutes, or until the spinach is wilted.

2. In a medium bowl, whisk together the eggs, salt, pepper, and nutmeg. Pour the mixture over the spinach in the skillet. Top evenly with peppers and cheese.

3. Using a spatula, carefully lift the edges to let the uncooked egg flow underneath. Continue this process until the frittata is almost set. Cover and cook for 2 more minutes or until frittata is set.

4. Serve the frittata cut into wedges and sprinkled with basil.

Serves 6. Prep time: 10 minutes. Cooking time: 10 minutes. Total time: 20 minutes.

....

Per serving: Calories: 165   Fat: 13.1g   Saturated Fat: 7.6g   Protein: 9.7g
Carbohydrates: 2.2g   Fiber: 0g

Hash Brown Scramble

This country-style dish contains a trifecta of breakfast favorites: tasty bacon, protein-packed eggs, and satisfying hash browns. For an added treat, top with grated Cheddar cheese or sprinkle with your favorite herb.

Ingredient Tip: Frozen hash browns are a terrific convenience item for use here or as a quick side dish for dinner. Check the label and make sure the only ingredient is potatoes. Some packaged hash browns have been coated in hydrogenated oils or other products to keep them from clumping together.

4 slices natural, uncured bacon	1 tablespoon avocado oil
6 eggs, beaten	2 cups frozen hash browns
½ teaspoon salt	½ cup chopped onion
½ teaspoon freshly ground black pepper	1 cup chopped tomatoes

1. In a large nonstick skillet over medium heat, cook the bacon until crisp. Remove the bacon and drain it on paper towels, reserving 2 tablespoons of drippings in pan. Crumble the bacon, and set aside.
2. Add the eggs, salt, and pepper to the skillet. Cook for 3 minutes, stirring to scramble. Remove the eggs from the skillet.
3. Heat the oil in the skillet; add the hash browns and onion. Sauté for 12 minutes or until the hash browns are browned and the onion is tender. Stir in the bacon, scrambled eggs, and tomato.
4. Mix the scramble gently in pan for 1 minute, just enough to cook the tomatoes slightly and warm up the eggs. Serve.

Serves 4. Prep time: 10 minutes. Cooking time: 20 minutes. Total time: 30 minutes.

. . . .

Per serving: Calories: 180   Fat: 9.8g   Saturated Fat: 3.1g   Protein: 11.9g
Carbohydrates: 11.8g   Fiber: 2.1g

Mini Spinach, Pepper, and Cheese Quiches

Little hand-held quiches are kid-friendly and can even be made in advance. By baking them in the muffin tins, it speeds up prep time and makes them a great grab-and-go breakfast. Feel free to add your favorite chopped vegetables or turkey sausage to make them even more delicious and nutritious.

1 tablespoon avocado oil, plus additional for greasing

1 red bell pepper, diced

4 cups chopped fresh baby spinach

6 eggs, lightly beaten

1 cup shredded sharp white Cheddar cheese

½ teaspoon salt

½ teaspoon freshly ground black pepper

1. Preheat the oven to 350°F.
2. Coat 8 cups of a muffin tin with the avocado oil.
3. Heat 1 tablespoon of avocado oil in a large skillet over medium-high heat. Add the bell pepper and spinach and cook, stirring frequently, for about 4 minutes or until the bell pepper begins to soften and the spinach is wilted. Transfer the mixture to a colander set over the sink to drain any excess liquid.
4. In a medium bowl, stir together the eggs, spinach–bell pepper mixture, cheese, salt, and pepper. Pour the mixture evenly into the prepared muffin tin cups.
5. Bake the muffins for 15 minutes or until the quiches are set. Let the quiches sit in the pan on a wire rack to cool slightly, about 5 minutes. Serve hot.

Serves 4. Prep time: 10 minutes. Cooking time: 20 minutes.
Total time: 30 minutes (plus 5 minutes to cool).

. . . .

Per serving: Calories: 230   Fat: 16.6g   Saturated Fat: 8.2g   Protein: 16.6g
Carbohydrates: 4.1g   Fiber: 1.5g

Scrambled Egg, Black Bean, and Avocado Breakfast Burritos

Breakfast burritos are convenient, hearty, and nutritious. They include protein from the eggs and beans, heart-healthy fat from the avocado, and fiber from the tortilla. They're perfect for a weekend meal or as take-along provisions during the week.

Ingredient Tip: Fresh salsa is an awesome condiment to buy prepared. Just be careful of added sugar lurking in the ingredients list. You should only find ingredients like tomatoes, cilantro, lime juice, and peppers.

1 tablespoon avocado oil

1 cup chopped red onion

1 (15-ounce) can black beans, drained and rinsed

6 eggs

½ teaspoon salt

½ teaspoon freshly ground black pepper

4 (100%) whole-grain tortillas, warmed

1 avocado, diced

½ cup Fresh Salsa (page 297)

½ cup shredded white Cheddar cheese

¼ cup chopped fresh cilantro

1. In a large nonstick skillet, heat the avocado oil over medium heat. Add the onion and cook for 5 minutes or until tender. Add the black beans and cook until warmed through, about 2 minutes. Remove the mixture from the skillet and keep warm.
2. In a medium bowl, whisk together the eggs, salt, and pepper. Add the eggs to the skillet, scrambling to cook through.
3. Spoon the onion mixture down the center of each tortilla, followed by the scrambled eggs. Top the eggs with avocado, salsa, cheese, and cilantro. Roll up and serve warm.

Serves 4. Prep time: 10 minutes. Cooking time: 10 minutes. Total time: 20 minutes.

Per serving: Calories: 723   Fat: 24.1g   Saturated Fat: 7.6g   Protein: 39.5g
Carbohydrates: 90.4g   Fiber: 22.9g

South-of-the-Border Breakfast Strata

Whether enjoyed for breakfast or dinner, this all-in-one meal covers all the major food groups. It also offers the convenience of being made ahead so all you have to do is pop a serving in the oven to warm when you are making your morning coffee.

1 cup Fresh Salsa (page 297)
1 cup canned black beans,
    drained and rinsed
8 slices frozen sprouted-grain
    bread, thawed and toasted
Coconut oil, for greasing
1 cup shredded sharp white
    Cheddar cheese

1 cup plain Greek yogurt
1 cup milk
½ teaspoon salt
½ teaspoon freshly ground
    black pepper
4 eggs
¼ cup chopped fresh cilantro

1. In a small bowl, combine the salsa and black beans. Set aside.
2. Cut the bread into cubes. In an 11-by-7-inch baking dish coated with coconut oil, arrange ⅓ of the bread cubes. Top with ⅓ cup of cheese and 1 cup of the salsa mixture.
3. Repeat the process with ⅓ of the bread, ⅓ cup of cheese, and the remaining 1 cup of salsa mixture; top with the remaining bread.
4. In a medium bowl, whisk together the yogurt, milk, salt, pepper, and eggs. Pour the mixture over the bread cubes; sprinkle with the remaining ⅓ cup of cheese. Cover and chill for 8 hours or overnight.
5. Preheat the oven to 350°F.
6. Remove the strata from the refrigerator and let it stand for 10 minutes. Cover with aluminum foil and bake for 20 minutes. Uncover and bake for 15 more minutes or until lightly browned and puffed.
7. Sprinkle with cilantro, cut into squares, and serve.

Serves 6. Prep time: 15 minutes. Cooking time: 35 minutes. Total time: 50 minutes (plus 8 hours to chill and 10 minutes to stand).

....
Per serving: Calories: 402   Fat: 13.1g   Saturated Fat: 6.5g   Protein: 24.6g
Carbohydrates: 51.1g   Fiber: 8.3g

6

Lunch

Curried Vegetable Soup

Curry, cilantro, ginger, and yogurt are ingredients found in the hot climates of India and Jamaica, which is why this soup features summer vegetables. The wisdom is that spiciness cools you off. The spiciness of the curry determines whether your soup will be mild, medium, or hot, so go with your palate.

Cooking Tip: Before pureeing the soup in the blender or food processor, remove the center hole in the lid to allow steam to escape. Process the soup in batches to prevent overflow.

2 tablespoons coconut oil
½ cup chopped red onion
2 garlic cloves, minced
1 tablespoon grated peeled
    fresh ginger
1 teaspoon curry powder
3 cups sliced zucchini and
    yellow squash, chopped
2 cups coarsely chopped
    fresh asparagus

5 cups reduced-sodium
    vegetable broth
½ teaspoon salt
½ teaspoon freshly ground
    black pepper
½ cup plain Greek yogurt
2 tablespoons chopped
    fresh cilantro

1. In a Dutch oven over medium-high heat, heat the coconut oil. Add the onion and cook, stirring frequently, for 5 minutes or until tender. Add the garlic, ginger, and curry powder, and stir to combine. Cook for 2 more minutes. Add the zucchini and yellow squash, and the asparagus, stirring to coat with the spices. Add the vegetable broth, salt, and pepper and stir to combine.
2. Cook for 10 minutes, or until the vegetables are tender. Pour the hot mixture into a blender or food processor, reserving half of the vegetables. Process until smooth. Return the soup to the Dutch oven. Stir in the reserved vegetables, yogurt, and cilantro. Cook for 1 to 2 minutes or until thoroughly heated through.
3. Serve hot in soup bowls.

Serves 4. Prep time: 10 minutes. Cooking time: 20 minutes. Total time: 30 minutes.

. . . .

Per serving: Calories: 179 Fat: 10g Saturated Fat: 7.2g Protein: 10.3g
Carbohydrates: 11.6g Fiber: 3g

Minestrone Soup

During the summer months, try adding green beans, when they're at their peak. Enjoy this delicious, hearty, traditional Italian soup for lunch or dinner. With protein from the beans and cheese, vitamins from lots of nutritious vegetables, and satisfying whole-grain pasta, it's a complete meal.

2 tablespoons coconut oil

1 onion, chopped

2 garlic cloves, minced

2 carrots, peeled and chopped

2 zucchini, halved lengthwise and thinly sliced

1 teaspoon dried oregano

1 (28-ounce) can whole tomatoes in puree, chopped

4 cups reduced-sodium vegetable broth

½ teaspoon salt

½ teaspoon freshly ground black pepper

1 (15-ounce) can kidney beans, drained and rinsed

1 cup frozen peas

1 cup uncooked 100% whole-wheat elbow pasta

½ cup freshly grated Parmesan cheese, for garnish

¼ cup chopped fresh basil, for garnish

1. In a large Dutch oven over medium heat, heat the oil. Add the onion and garlic. Cook for 5 minutes or until tender.
2. Add the carrots; cook for 5 more minutes or until the carrots have softened.
3. Stir in the zucchini, oregano, tomatoes, broth, salt, and pepper. Bring to a boil. Reduce the heat to medium-low and simmer for 10 minutes.
4. Stir in the kidney beans, peas, and pasta. Cook for 10 minutes or until the pasta is tender. Garnish each serving with cheese and basil.

Serves 4. Prep time: 10 minutes. Cooking time: 30 minutes. Total time: 40 minutes.

....

Per serving: Calories: 739   Fat: 12.5g   Saturated Fat: 7.9g   Protein: 40.8g
Carbohydrates: 119.2g   Fiber: 26.8g

Corn and Potato Chowder

This soup offers comfort in a bowl and is perfect any time of year. With fresh sweet kernels of corn and chunks of potato, it's a hearty soup that makes a satisfying meal when paired with a side salad or sprouted-grain bread. Add a garnish of fresh chives if you like.

Cooking Tip: Be sure to cut the potatoes into even chunks so that they'll all cook evenly.

2 tablespoons avocado oil

½ cup chopped onion

1½ cups fresh corn kernels
   (about 3 corn ears)

1 cup milk

1 (14.5-ounce) can reduced-
   sodium vegetable broth

½ pound new potatoes, diced

½ teaspoon salt

½ teaspoon freshly ground
   black pepper

¼ cup sour cream, for garnish

1. Heat the oil in a Dutch oven over medium-high heat. Add the onion and corn and cook, stirring frequently, for 5 minutes or until the onion and corn are tender.

2. Add the milk, broth, potatoes, salt, and pepper. Bring to a boil. Reduce the heat and simmer for 15 minutes or until the potatoes are tender. Mash the mixture with a potato masher to reach the desired consistency.

3. Serve hot, garnished with a dollop of sour cream.

Serves 4. Prep time: 10 minutes. Cooking time: 20 minutes. Total time: 30 minutes.

. . . .

Per serving: Calories: 230   Fat: 12.1g   Saturated Fat: 3.8g   Protein: 7.1g
Carbohydrates: 25.5g   Fiber: 3.1g

Black Bean Soup

Enjoy this satisfying soup hot or cold. The fresh salsa is the perfect flavor complement for the black beans. By mashing one of the cans of beans in the recipe, you'll provide a natural thickener to the base. Or you can omit this step if you like a thinner soup.

Time-Saving Tip: If you don't have time to make the fresh salsa, you can purchase it in the deli department of your grocery store. Check the label first to make sure there is no added sugar.

2 tablespoons avocado oil

2 garlic cloves, minced

1 teaspoon ground cumin

1 teaspoon chili powder

3 (15.5-ounce) cans black
    beans, drained and rinsed

1 (14.5-ounce) can reduced-
    sodium vegetable broth

2 cups Fresh Salsa (page 297)

2 tablespoons lime juice

¼ cup chopped fresh cilantro

1. In a large Dutch oven, heat the oil over medium heat; add the garlic, cumin, and chili powder. Cook for 2 minutes or until the garlic is tender.
2. Mash one can of black beans with a potato masher.
3. Add the black beans, broth, and salsa to the spices in the Dutch oven. Cook for 10 minutes or until the soup is thoroughly heated. Stir in the lime juice and cilantro.
4. Serve the soup hot.

Serves 4. Prep time: 5 minutes. Cooking time: 15 minutes. Total time: 20 minutes.

Per serving: Calories: 1,197   Fat: 6.6g   Saturated Fat: 1.6g   Protein: 75.7g
Carbohydrates: 217.4g   Fiber: 52.9g

Three-Bean Farro Salad

This tangy bean salad is the perfect lunch, packed with healthy fiber and protein to get you through your day. Farro is an ancient super-grain that has a nutty flavor and is a good source of iron in addition to fiber and protein. It is easy to digest and a delicious alternative to brown rice.

On-the-Go Tip: This salad can be made ahead as a take-along lunch, as the flavors actually improve over time. Make it the night before and store in an airtight container.

1 cup farro

1 (15-ounce) can kidney beans, drained and rinsed

1 (15.5-ounce) can chickpeas, drained and rinsed

2 cups coarsely chopped cooked green beans

¼ cup finely chopped red onion

¼ cup crumbled feta cheese

½ cup Mustard-Thyme Vinaigrette (page 303)

1. Cook the farro according to the package directions; rinse with cold water.
2. Combine the farro, kidney beans, chickpeas, green beans, red onion, and feta cheese in a medium bowl.
3. Pour the dressing over the farro mixture, tossing to coat.
4. Serve at room temperature.

Serves 4. Prep time: 10 minutes. Cooking time: 15 minutes. Total time: 25 minutes.

. . . .

Per serving: Calories: 998 Fat: 11g Saturated Fat: 2.3g Protein: 54.8g
Carbohydrates: 177g Fiber: 42.6g

Chicken-Quinoa Salad with Oranges, Olives, and Feta

This delicious chicken salad is a tasty, complete meal of protein, nutty grain, and sweet oranges. Quinoa is one of the few plant foods that's a complete protein, and it has an unusually high ratio of protein to carbohydrates. Try using it in place of rice. Just be sure to rinse it before cooking to remove the natural saponin, the plant's defense against pests, because it leaves a bitter taste.

Ingredient Variations: Quinoa is the perfect base for just about any salad, and the longer it stands, the more it soaks up the flavors. Try it with your favorite vinaigrette and chopped tomatoes, fresh basil, fresh mozzarella, and olives for an Italian flavor. Or try a Mexican approach with avocado, fresh salsa, fresh cilantro, and fajita steak slices.

1¼ cups quinoa

3 cups shredded
    cooked chicken

1 garlic clove, minced

3 oranges, peeled
    and sectioned

½ cup pitted green
    olives, halved

½ cup crumbled feta cheese

¼ cup lime juice

¼ cup chopped fresh cilantro

2 tablespoons extra-virgin
    olive oil

½ teaspoon salt

½ teaspoon freshly ground
    black pepper

1. Cook the quinoa according to the package directions. In a wire-mesh strainer, rinse under cold water to cool.
2. Combine the quinoa, chicken, garlic, oranges, olives, and feta cheese in a large bowl.
3. In a small bowl, whisk together the lime juice, cilantro, oil, salt, and pepper; pour the dressing over the quinoa mixture, tossing to coat well, and serve.

Serves 4. Prep time: 10 minutes. Cooking time: 15 minutes. Total time: 25 minutes.

....

Per serving: Calories: 550   Fat: 18.7g   Saturated Fat: 4.2g   Protein: 47.3g
Carbohydrates: 49.7g   Fiber: 6.9g

Tuna-Barley Salad with Roasted Red Peppers and Artichokes

Take a trip to the Mediterranean with this heart-healthy tuna salad with delicious fresh vegetables and barley. Barley is a tasty cereal grain that helps control blood sugar, reduces blood pressure and cholesterol, and may even help with weight control. It is nutty in flavor and a great alternative to rice.

Make-Ahead Tip: The flavor of this salad improves over time, so make it the night before to pack in your bag the following day.

1½ cups uncooked barley

1 (12-ounce) jar artichoke hearts, drained and coarsely chopped

1 (12-ounce) jar roasted red peppers, drained and coarsely chopped

3 cups chopped fresh baby spinach

2 (5-ounce) cans albacore tuna in water, drained and flaked

3 tablespoons extra-virgin olive oil

2 tablespoons lemon juice

1 tablespoon chopped fresh basil

½ teaspoon salt

½ teaspoon freshly ground black pepper

1. Cook the barley according to the package directions, then drain; rinse under cold water to cool.
2. In a large bowl, combine the barley, artichokes, peppers, spinach, and tuna.
3. In a small bowl, whisk together the oil, lemon juice, basil, salt, and pepper; pour the dressing over the barley mixture. Toss gently to coat and serve.

Serves 4. Prep time: 10 minutes. Cooking time: 20 minutes. Total time: 30 minutes.

. . . .

Per serving: Calories: 492   Fat: 13g   Saturated Fat: 2.1g   Protein: 30.2g
Carbohydrates: 63.5g   Fiber: 17.1g

Creamy Asparagus Soup

One of the first signs of spring, asparagus is one of the best super-foods you can eat. It's loaded with fiber, vitamins A, C, E, and K, and folate. This delicious creamy soup is wonderful served either warm or cold. Try it with a dollop of yogurt.

Ingredient Tip: If you like your soup to have more texture, leave out one-quarter of the chopped asparagus when pureeing and then stir it in at the end.

2 tablespoons avocado oil

2 garlic cloves, minced

2 pounds fresh asparagus, coarsely chopped

4 cups reduced-sodium vegetable broth

½ cup plain Greek yogurt

½ teaspoon salt

½ teaspoon freshly ground black pepper

1. In a Dutch oven, heat the oil over medium heat; add the garlic and asparagus. Sauté for 3 minutes. Add the broth; cover and cook for 5 minutes or until the asparagus is tender.
2. Process the soup in batches in a blender or food processor until smooth. Return the soup to the Dutch oven. Stir in the yogurt, salt, and pepper. Cook over medium heat for 5 minutes or until the soup is thickened. Serve hot.

Serves 4. Prep time: 15 minutes. Cooking time: 15 minutes. Total time: 30 minutes.

Per serving: Calories: 122   Fat: 3.8g   Saturated Fat: 1.4g   Protein: 12.4g
Carbohydrates: 12g   Fiber: 5.2g

Southwestern Salad with Shrimp and Black Beans

This salad is a fiesta in a bowl. With plump shrimp, fresh corn kernels, and black beans, dressed with a cilantro-lime vinaigrette, it will satisfy your taste buds from lunch until dinner. Store the leftover canned black beans in an airtight container in the fridge. You can stir them into salsa, top another salad with the extra, or use it in several other recipes in the book.

Ingredient Tip: To get 1 pound of shrimp, peeled and deveined, buy an extra ¼ pound to account for the weight of the shells. To save time, buy the shrimp already peeled and deveined.

1 pound peeled and deveined
　　large shrimp

½ teaspoon chili powder

½ teaspoon ground cumin

½ teaspoon salt

½ teaspoon freshly ground
　　black pepper

1 tablespoon avocado oil

1 cup fresh corn kernels
　　(2 ears corn)

6 cups chopped
　　romaine lettuce

2 tomatoes, chopped

1 avocado, diced

1 cup canned black beans,
　　drained and rinsed

⅓ cup Cilantro-Lime
　　Vinaigrette (page 302)

1. Sprinkle the shrimp with chili powder, cumin, salt, and pepper.
2. Heat the oil in a large nonstick skillet over medium-high heat; add the shrimp. Sauté for 3 minutes or until the shrimp are done. Remove the shrimp from the skillet.
3. Add the corn to the skillet; sauté for 5 minutes or until tender.
4. In a large bowl, combine the lettuce, tomatoes, avocado, and black beans. Add the shrimp and corn. Add dressing, tossing well to coat.
5. Serve. Garnish with a slice of lime if you desire.

Serves 4. Prep time: 10 minutes. Cooking time: 10 minutes. Total time: 20 minutes.

. . . .

Per serving:　Calories: 474　Fat: 16.6g　Saturated Fat: 2.4g　Protein: 31.9g
Carbohydrates: 57.1g　Fiber: 13.7g

Almond Butter–Apple Sandwiches

Vegan

These sandwiches are kid-friendly and can be enjoyed as a snack. Apples and almond butter are tasty companions for this adventuresome sandwich. Explore the many great apple choices at the store. If you like tart apples, Granny Smith are great. Golden Delicious apples are sweet and tender, and Fuji apples are sweet and crisp.

Ingredient Variation: Nut butters are readily available at many grocery stores, and it's fun to experiment with different types. Try cashew butter or our recipe for Creamy Natural Peanut Butter (page 306) in place of the almond butter. You may switch out sliced banana slices for the apple, too, if you'd like.

8 tablespoons all-natural almond butter

8 slices frozen sprouted-grain bread, thawed and toasted

1 apple, thinly sliced

4 tablespoons honey

¼ teaspoon ground cinnamon

1. Spread 1 tablespoon of the almond butter onto one side of each slice of bread.
2. Arrange the apple slices over the almond butter in one layer on four slices of bread. Drizzle 1 tablespoon of honey over the apples and sprinkle with cinnamon.
3. Top with the remaining apple butter bread slices, and serve.

Serves 4. Prep time: 10 minutes.

....

Per serving: Calories: 428   Fat: 16.1g   Saturated Fat: 1g   Protein: 15.1g
Carbohydrates: 59.9g   Fiber: 11.2g

Turkey-Cucumber Sandwiches with Mashed Avocado

Tangy mashed avocado makes a delicious spread for these turkey sandwiches. Topped with crisp cucumber, this sandwich hits every texture note. If you have leftover cooked chicken, it substitutes well for the turkey.

Ingredient Tip: Avocado is a star ingredient in this dish, so be sure to choose the best one at the grocery store. Often times they are rock hard, so to speed up ripening, place them in a brown paper bag with an apple or banana. To determine if they are ready to eat, gently press the stem end with your thumb; if it depresses easily, your avocado is ripe.

1 avocado, mashed

1 tablespoon lime juice

¼ teaspoon salt

¼ teaspoon freshly ground black pepper

8 slices frozen sprouted-grain bread, thawed and toasted

1 cucumber, thinly sliced

¼ cup fresh basil leaves

1 (7-ounce) sliced natural, deli-roasted turkey (no nitrates)

1. In a small bowl, stir together the avocado, lime juice, salt, and pepper; spread the mixture evenly on four bread slices.
2. Top the unused bread slices with the cucumber, basil, and turkey. Place the four avocado-topped bread slices on top of the turkey. Serve.

Serves 4. Prep time: 10 minutes.

....

Per serving: Calories: 321 Fat: 11.3g Saturated Fat: 2.1g Protein: 17.9g
Carbohydrates: 44.1g Fiber: 7.9g

Pasta Salad with Avocado-Pesto Cream Sauce

Who knew avocados were so versatile? Here they are used to make a decadent, creamy pasta sauce, without the bad fat associated with conventional cream sauces. If you make this one ahead, don't worry if the sauce turns a bit brown from the avocados. It's still as delicious to eat.

On-the-Go Tip: This lunch pasta salad is great to make and take with you. If you make it ahead, add a little warm water before serving to loosen up the sauce a bit.

12 ounces 100% whole-wheat fusilli

2 avocados, coarsely chopped

3 tablespoons lemon juice

3 tablespoons Basil Pesto (page 292)

1 tablespoon extra-virgin olive oil

¼ teaspoon salt

1 cup chopped tomatoes

½ cup freshly grated Parmesan cheese

1. Cook the pasta according to the package directions; drain and rinse under cold water to cool.
2. In a food processor, combine the avocados, lemon juice, pesto, oil, and salt; process until smooth.
3. In a large bowl, combine the pasta, tomatoes, and avocado sauce. Sprinkle each serving with cheese.

Serves 4. Prep time: 10 minutes. Cooking time: 20 minutes. Total time: 30 minutes.
....

Per serving: Calories: 564   Fat: 28.6g   Saturated Fat: 6.7g   Protein: 19.1g
Carbohydrates: 64g   Fiber: 17.9

Beef and Goat Cheese Quesadillas

The combination of shredded beef and crumbled goat cheese is a heavenly flavor match. This recipe takes advantage of any leftover pot roast or beef you may have from earlier in the week. If you don't have leftovers, you can grill a piece of beef and then slice it. Or, use shredded deli-roasted chicken in place of the beef.

Perfect Pair: For added flavor and south-of-the-border flair, serve these quesadillas with a dollop of Chunky Guacamole (page 300).

4 (100%) whole-wheat tortillas

3 cups shredded cooked beef

1 cup jarred sliced roasted
    red peppers

½ cup canned roasted green
    chiles, sliced

1 cup crumbled goat cheese

2 tablespoons avocado oil

1 lime, cut into wedges,
    for garnish

1. Layer one half of each tortilla with the beef, peppers, and green chiles, dividing the ingredients evenly. Top each tortilla with ¼ cup of crumbled goat cheese. Fold the tortillas over to create half-moons.
2. In a large skillet, heat 1 tablespoon of oil over medium heat. Place two tortillas in the skillet. Cook them for 2 to 3 minutes on each side or until browned and the filling is warm.
3. Repeat with the remaining tortillas.
4. Cut the quesadillas into wedges before serving. Serve the quesadillas hot, garnished with lime wedges.

Serves 4. Prep time: 10 minutes. Cooking time: 10 minutes. Total time: 20 minutes.

Per serving: Calories: 366   Fat: 17.1g   Saturated Fat: 9.3g   Protein: 36.5g
Carbohydrates: 15.8g   Fiber: 2.5g

Mediterranean Turkey Wrap

This recipe uses mayonnaise stirred with a little basil and feta cheese to create a delicious herb spread. Some specialty health food stores may have a clean version of mayonnaise, but it can be hard to find. It's very easy to make homemade mayonnaise and it can last for up to a week in the refrigerator.

Cooking Tip: This recipe calls for "lightly packed" spinach. Instead of pressing the spinach in the measuring cup, let it layer naturally. Otherwise, you may have too much and your wrap may be too full to roll.

¼ cup Homemade Mayonnaise (page 288)

2 tablespoons chopped fresh basil

2 tablespoons crumbled feta cheese

4 frozen sprouted-grain tortillas, thawed

3 cups lightly packed fresh baby spinach

2 jarred roasted red peppers, thinly sliced

7 ounces sliced natural, deli-roasted turkey (no nitrates)

1. In a small bowl, stir together the mayonnaise, basil, and feta cheese.
2. Spread the mayonnaise mixture evenly on one side of each tortilla. Top evenly with spinach, peppers, and turkey. Roll up, jelly-roll style, and secure with wooden toothpicks. Serve.

Serves 4. Prep time: 10 minutes.

Per serving: Calories: 219   Fat: 7g   Saturated Fat: 1.4g   Protein: 14.9g
Carbohydrates: 20.5g   Fiber: 2.5g

Chicken-Pesto BLT

The classic BLT gets an update with chicken and homemade pesto in this tasty sandwich. Use leftover chicken from a meal earlier in the week, or buy a sliced roasted natural chicken at the grocery store deli for convenience.

Ingredient Variation: There are so many great options for changing up this sandwich. Try roast beef slices, a piece of grilled salmon, or even flaked tuna.

¼ cup Basil Pesto (page 292)

8 slices frozen sprouted-grain bread, thawed and toasted

6 slices natural, cooked uncured bacon

3 cups sliced cooked chicken breast

2 tomatoes, sliced

4 romaine lettuce leaves

1. Spread the pesto on one side of each piece of bread. Top four of the bread slices with 1½ slices of cooked bacon, ¾ cup of chicken, ¼ of the tomato slices, and 1 lettuce leaf.
2. Top the lettuce with the remaining bread slices and serve.

Serves 4. Prep time: 10 minutes.

. . . .

Per serving: Calories: 469   Fat: 14.5g   Saturated Fat: 2.8g   Protein: 49.3g
Carbohydrates: 33.5g   Fiber: 7.1g

7

Snacks

Herbed Pita Chips

Pita chips are so easy to make, and making them yourself helps you know you're eating clean. Whether served with one of the many homemade dips in this book or served with store-bought hummus, everyone will love these herbed chips.

Cooking Tip: Use a large knife and cutting board to cut the pitas quickly into triangles. Separating the triangles before baking makes the chips extra-crispy.

4 (100%) whole-grain pitas

3 tablespoons coconut oil, melted

1 tablespoon Italian seasoning

½ teaspoon salt

½ teaspoon freshly ground black pepper

1. Preheat the oven to 400°F.
2. Cut the pitas into 6 triangles. Separate the triangles.
3. Put the pita triangles on a rimmed baking sheet and brush them with the coconut oil. Sprinkle the pita triangles evenly with the Italian seasoning, salt, and pepper.
4. Bake for 8 to 10 minutes or until the pita chips are brown and crispy.
5. Let the chips cool. Serve.

Serves 6. Prep time: 10 minutes. Cooking time: 10 minutes. Total time: 20 minutes.

. . . .

Per serving: Calories: 171   Fat: 8.2g   Saturated Fat: 6g   Protein: 4g
Carbohydrates: 21g   Fiber: 2.1g

Baked Tortilla Chips

These crunchy chips are simple to prepare and are the perfect accompaniment to Fresh Salsa (page 297) or Chunky Guacamole (page 300). Because they are baked, they're low in fat, but they're still crisp and will scoop up your favorite dips effortlessly.

Cooking Tip: Don't be tempted to crowd the pan with the tortilla wedges. Baking them in single layers allows the chips to crisp up. Bake them in two batches, if needed.

2 tablespoons coconut oil, for greasing

6 (8-inch) 100% whole-wheat tortillas

¼ teaspoon salt

1. Preheat the oven to 425°F.
2. Coat a rimmed baking sheet with coconut oil.
3. Cut each tortilla into 8 wedges; brush the wedges evenly with the coconut oil and sprinkle with salt.
4. Arrange tortillas in one layer on the prepared baking sheet. Bake for 8 minutes or until crisp.
5. Let the chips cool. Serve.

Serves 8. Prep time: 10 minutes. Cooking time: 10 minutes. Total time: 20 minutes.

Per serving: Calories: 127   Fat: 5.3g   Saturated Fat: 2.9g   Protein: 3.8g
Carbohydrates: 18g   Fiber: 3g

Sweet and Spicy Nuts

These perfectly seasoned mixed nuts may become addictive. With just the right amount of sweet honey and tangy spices, they will become one of your favorite snacks. To prevent yourself from eating the whole batch in one sitting, portion out servings into zip-top plastic bags or small containers.

Double It: These nuts stay fresh for a long time so do yourself a favor and make enough for snacks for a while. They also make a great gift around the holidays.

2 egg whites

3 tablespoons honey

8 ounces raw pecan halves

4 ounces raw cashews

4 ounces whole almonds

2 ounces toasted
   sunflower seeds

1 teaspoon chili powder

1 teaspoon ground cinnamon

½ teaspoon salt

½ teaspoon cayenne pepper

1. Preheat the oven to 300°F.
2. Line a rimmed baking sheet with parchment paper.
3. In a large bowl, whisk the egg whites until foamy; whisk in the honey until combined.
4. Add the pecan halves, cashews, almonds, and sunflower seeds to the bowl; toss until coated with the egg white mixture. Add the chili powder, cinnamon, salt, and cayenne pepper. Toss thoroughly until evenly distributed.
5. With a slotted spoon, transfer the mixture to the prepared baking sheet. Bake the nuts for 25 minutes or until they are browned and the coating is dry.
6. Let the nuts cool on the baking sheet for 20 minutes before serving. Store the nuts in an airtight container for up to 2 weeks.

Makes 4 cups. Prep time: 10 minutes. Cooking time: 25 minutes.
Total time: 35 minutes (plus 20 minutes to cool).

. . . .

Per serving (¼ cup):   Calories: 234   Fat: 20.5g   Saturated Fat: 3.6g   Protein: 5.4g
Carbohydrates: 10.8g   Fiber: 3.2g

Crunchy Cumin-Spiced Chickpeas

These crunchy, tasty chickpeas are guaranteed to become your next favorite snack. They are quick to prepare and great to have on hand to add to salads or just grab by the handful. Experiment with other dried spices for a different taste treat.

Storage Tip: Be sure to store these chickpeas in an airtight container so they don't lose their crunchiness. If they become soft, pop them in the oven for 5 minutes to recrisp.

2 (15.5-ounce) cans chickpeas,
    drained and rinsed
2 tablespoons coconut oil

2 teaspoons ground cumin
1 teaspoon garlic powder
½ teaspoon salt

1. Preheat the oven to 400°F.
2. Line a rimmed baking sheet with parchment paper. Place the chickpeas on a paper towel and dry completely.
3. In a large bowl, combine the chickpeas, coconut oil, cumin, garlic powder, and salt. Spread the chickpeas into one layer on the prepared baking sheet.
4. Bake for 40 to 45 minutes, turning occasionally, until the chickpeas are lightly browned and crispy. Remove the chickpeas from the oven and let them cool completely.
5. Serve or store in an airtight container for 3 days.

Makes about 3 1/2 cups. Prep time: 5 minutes. Cooking time: 40 minutes. Total time: 45 minutes.

. . . .

Per serving (¼ cup): Calories: 247   Fat: 6g   Saturated Fat: 2.1g   Protein: 12.2g   Carbohydrates: 38.4g   Fiber: 11g

Cranberry, Cinnamon, and Oat Bars

These homemade granola bars are great for tucking in your purse or into lunch boxes. They call for homemade peanut butter, but feel free to purchase natural peanut butter or almond butter at the market if you are pressed for time.

Storage Tip: For convenience, you can make these no-bake granola bars and keep them stored, wrapped snugly in plastic wrap and tucked into zip-top freezer bags, in the freezer for up to 1 month.

⅓ cup coconut oil, plus additional for greasing

2 cups uncooked old-fashioned rolled oats

½ cup dried unsweetened cranberries

2 teaspoons ground cinnamon

⅓ cup honey

¾ cup Creamy Natural Peanut Butter (page 306)

1 teaspoon pure vanilla extract

1. Coat an 8-inch baking pan with coconut oil.
2. In a large bowl, combine the oats, cranberries, and cinnamon.
3. In a medium saucepan, combine the ⅓ cup coconut oil, honey, and peanut butter. Cook over medium-low heat, just until melted, about 5 minutes. Stir in the vanilla.
4. Pour the mixture evenly over the oat mixture, tossing well to coat completely.
5. Press mixture into the prepared pan. Refrigerate the mixture for 3 hours, or until firm. Cut into bars. Store, wrapped with plastic wrap, in the refrigerator for up to 1 week.

Serves 8. Prep time: 10 minutes. Cooking time: 5 minutes.
Total time: 15 minutes (plus 3 hours to chill).

. . . .

Per serving: Calories: 374   Fat: 22.6g   Saturated Fat: 10.1g   Protein: 9.3g
Carbohydrates: 36.4g   Fiber: 4.2g

Spiced Pecan-Almond Granola with Dried Fruit

Homemade granola is easy to make, and this one is particularly delicious. It's a tasty combination of oats, nuts, fruit, and spices and a totally satisfying way to start your day off with energy. And oats are a great source of soluble fiber—the type that helps block the absorption of cholesterol.

Storage Tip: This granola is great to have on-hand for cereal, yogurt parfait, or snacking by the handful. Keep it stored in an airtight container for up to 1 week.

2 cups uncooked old-fashioned
   rolled oats
½ cup chopped pecans
½ cup chopped almonds
⅓ cup pumpkin seeds
1 teaspoon ground cinnamon
¼ teaspoon allspice

1 tablespoon coconut oil
¼ cup pure maple syrup
2 tablespoons honey
¼ cup unsweetened
   dried cranberries
¼ cup chopped dried apricots

1. Preheat the oven to 300°F.
2. In a large bowl, combine the oats, pecans, almonds, pumpkin seeds, cinnamon, and allspice.
3. In a small bowl, combine the coconut oil, maple syrup, and honey. Add the wet ingredients to the oat mixture, tossing well to coat.
4. Pour the mixture into a single layer on a rimmed baking sheet. Bake for 20 minutes; then stir. Bake for 15 to 20 more minutes or until the granola is toasted. Remove the granola from the oven and let cool. Break the granola into chunks. Stir in the cranberries and apricots.
5. Serve with milk or almond milk, over yogurt, or plain as a snack.

Makes 4 cups. Prep time: 10 minutes. Cooking time: 35 minutes. Total time: 45 minutes.

Per serving (½ cup):   Calories: 192   Fat: 7.9g   Saturated Fat: 2.4g   Protein: 4.8g
Carbohydrates: 27.6g   Fiber: 3.1g

Salt and Pepper Kale Chips

Vegan
Gluten-Free
Dairy-Free

Kale is a superfood that has made waves in recent nutrition news. If you've got a craving for potato chips, you will find this crispy snack very satisfying. Kale is one of the healthiest vegetables on the planet and is known for helping prevent cancer and lowering cholesterol. But with this delicious snack, you won't realize you're eating something healthy.

Ingredient Tip: For the best result, buy bunches of fresh kale instead of the pre-chopped variety. They tend to be fresher and will produce a better result.

2 tablespoons avocado oil, plus additional for greasing

1 pound kale

½ teaspoon salt

½ teaspoon freshly ground black pepper

1. Preheat the oven to 350°F.
2. Brush two rimmed baking sheets with oil.
3. Remove the center rib and stems from the kale; tear the leaves into 2-inch pieces.
4. Place the kale in a large bowl; add 2 tablespoons of oil, salt, and pepper. Toss well to coat.
5. Arrange the kale in a single layer on the baking sheets.
6. Bake for 12 to 15 minutes or until the edges are browned and the kale is crisp.
7. Let cool. Serve or store in an airtight container.

Serves 8. Prep time: 10 minutes. Cooking time: 15 minutes. Total time: 25 minutes.

. . . .

Per serving: Calories: 33   Fat: 0.4g   Saturated Fat: 0g   Protein: 1.7g
Carbohydrates: 6.2g   Fiber: 1g

Garlic-Herb Popcorn

Vegan
Gluten-Free
Dairy-Free

This low-calorie, healthy snack is just the ticket when you are craving something crunchy and salty. Buy organic popcorn kernels that are not genetically modified, and cook them on the stove top instead of in the microwave.

Ingredient Variations: The different flavor combinations to try with popcorn are endless. Try a cheesy version with grated Parmesan cheese and freshly ground pepper. Or go for a sweet popcorn with unsweetened cocoa powder and coconut sugar.

2 tablespoons coconut oil
½ cup organic popcorn kernels
1 tablespoon garlic powder

1 tablespoon Italian seasoning
½ teaspoon salt

1. In a large pot over high heat, add the oil and popcorn kernels. Cook, covered, swirling the pan occasionally, until the popcorn begins to pop slowly.
2. Remove the pan from the heat and keep it covered until the popcorn finishes popping.
3. Add the garlic powder, Italian seasoning, and salt to the popcorn, tossing to coat. Serve.

Serves 4. Prep time: 5 minutes. Cooking time: 10 minutes. Total time: 15 minutes.

Per serving: Calories: 81   Fat: 8g   Saturated Fat: 6.1g   Protein: 0.4g
Carbohydrates: 2.5g   Fiber: 0g

Beet Chips with Creamy Goat Cheese Dip

You will feel like a gourmet chef when you make this delicious snack. Beets are packed with blood pressure–lowering properties, they boost stamina in workouts, they fight inflammation, and they help your body detoxify. When you pair beets with goat cheese, you will be in taste bud heaven.

Ingredient Tip: A mandoline is especially helpful in slicing the beets super-thin.

For the chips:

1 tablespoon coconut oil, plus more for greasing

2 beets, peeled

¼ teaspoon salt

¼ teaspoon freshly ground black pepper

For the dip:

3 ounces goat cheese, softened

⅓ cup plain Greek yogurt

1 garlic clove, minced

1 tablespoon lemon juice

1 tablespoon milk

½ teaspoon dried thyme

¼ teaspoon salt

¼ teaspoon freshly ground black pepper

To make the chips:

1. Preheat the oven to 350°F.
2. Brush two rimmed baking sheets with coconut oil.
3. Cut the beets into very thin slices. Place the beets in a large bowl, and toss them with 1 tablespoon of coconut oil, salt, and pepper.
4. Arrange the beets in one layer on the baking sheets. Place one pan in the upper third of the oven and the other in the bottom third.
5. Bake for 20 minutes, or until the edges begin to dry out. Rotate the pans and bake for 10 to 15 more minutes, or until the edges begin to brown.
6. Transfer the beets to a wire rack; they will crisp up as they cool.

To make the dip:

1. In a food processor, combine the goat cheese, yogurt, garlic, lemon juice, milk, thyme, salt, and pepper; process until smooth.
2. Serve the dip alongside the chips. Store the dip in an airtight container for up to 1 week.

Serves 4. Prep time: 15 minutes. Cooking time: 30 minutes. Total time: 45 minutes.

. . . .

Per serving: Calories: 170   Fat: 12g   Saturated Fat: 8.8g   Protein: 9.1g
Carbohydrates: 7g   Fiber: 1.2g

Tabbouleh

This traditional Middle Eastern dish is perfect as a snack or as a quick side dish or lunch. The fresh parsley and mint give it a refreshing flavor, and the fiber from the bulgur helps you stay full when the afternoon slump hits.

Ingredient Tip: As the cucumber and tomatoes stand, they will release some of their juices naturally. If you make this dish ahead of time, use a slotted spoon to serve it onto plates.

½ cup bulgur wheat

3 tablespoons extra-virgin
   olive oil

1 cup chopped fresh parsley

½ cup chopped fresh mint

2 tomatoes, chopped

1 small cucumber, peeled and
   finely chopped

¼ cup finely chopped red onion

Juice and zest of 1 lemon

½ teaspoon salt

½ teaspoon freshly ground
   black pepper

1. Prepare the bulgur wheat according to the package directions; drain and rinse under cold water to cool.
2. In a large bowl, combine the bulgur, oil, parsley, mint, tomatoes, cucumber, red onion, lemon juice and zest, salt, and pepper.
3. Serve or store in an airtight container in the refrigerator for up to 3 days.

Serves 6. Prep time: 10 minutes.

. . . .

Per serving: Calories: 127   Fat: 7.5g   Saturated Fat: 1.1g   Protein: 2.8g
Carbohydrates: 15g   Fiber: 4.2g

Roasted Carrot Dip

Carrots are one of the healthiest foods you can eat and are available year-round. Carrots are packed with beta-carotene and have wonderful antioxidizing benefits. As if that weren't enough, they also help protect against cardiovascular disease and colon cancer. But they're not just good for you. When roasted, they offer a rich, sweet taste to this delicious spicy dip.

Perfect Pair: Serve this dip with pita chips. The recipe for homemade Herbed Pita Chips (page 132) is an easy one, but sometimes it's difficult to spare even an extra ten minutes. Instead, add 100% whole-grain pita chips to your grocery list. Clean pita chips are available in grocery stores.

2 tablespoons coconut oil, plus additional for greasing

1½ pounds carrots

1 large red onion, cut into wedges

2 tablespoons coconut oil

1½ teaspoons ground cumin

½ teaspoon salt

2 tablespoons lemon juice

2 garlic cloves, minced

3 tablespoons extra-virgin olive oil

1. Preheat the oven to 425°F.
2. Brush a rimmed baking sheet with coconut oil.
3. In a medium bowl, combine the carrots and onion with coconut oil, cumin, and salt. Spread the mixture on the prepared baking sheet.
4. Bake for 35 minutes, turning once, until the carrots are browned and tender.
5. Transfer the mixture to a food processor; add the lemon juice, garlic, and extra-virgin olive oil. Pulse until smooth.

Makes about 2 ½ cups. Prep time: 15 minutes. Cooking time: 35 minutes. Total time: 50 minutes.

. . . .

Per serving (2 tablespoons): Calories: 48 Fat: 3.5g Saturated Fat: 1.5g
Protein: 0.4g Carbohydrates: 4.2g Fiber: 1g Sodium: 82mg

Creamy Spinach-Artichoke Dip

Hooray! It's possible to enjoy this party-food favorite and still eat clean. Whether scooped up with Baked Tortilla Chips (page 133), Herbed Pita Chips (page 132), or fresh-cut veggies, you can't go wrong with this tasty, healthy, creamy spinach-artichoke dip.

Cooking Tip: If you like your spinach-artichoke dip hot, this one can be heated up in the oven. Spoon the dip into a shallow baking dish and bake at 350°F for 20 to 25 minutes or until bubbly.

2 garlic cloves, chopped

1 (8-ounce) package cream cheese, softened

1 cup plain Greek yogurt

2 tablespoons lemon juice

¼ cup freshly grated Parmesan cheese

½ teaspoon salt

½ teaspoon freshly ground black pepper

1 (10-ounce) package frozen chopped spinach, thawed and drained well

1 (12-ounce) jar artichoke hearts, drained

1. In a food processor, pulse the garlic, cream cheese, yogurt, lemon juice, Parmesan cheese, salt, and pepper until combined.
2. Add the spinach and artichokes. Pulse to the desired smoothness. Serve or store in an airtight container for up to 3 days.

Makes 2½ cups. Prep time: 10 minutes.

Per serving (¼ cup):   Calories: 134   Fat: 9.7g   Saturated Fat: 6g   Protein: 6.5g
Carbohydrates: 6.6g   Fiber: 2.5g   Sodium: 275mg

White Bean Hummus

Vegan
Gluten-Free

Hummus is one of the easiest snacks to make, and there are so many variations you can create. One key ingredient in hummus is tahini paste—ground sesame seeds, which gives the dip its distinctive Middle Eastern flavor. You can find tahini at virtually every grocery store in either the nut butter aisle or the international foods aisle.

Serving Tip: Serve this dip with fresh-cut veggies or Herbed Pita Chips (page 132).

2 garlic cloves

1 (15.5-ounce) can cannellini
    beans, drained and rinsed

4 tablespoons extra-virgin
    olive oil

3 tablespoons lemon juice

3 tablespoons tahini

½ teaspoon dried oregano

¼ teaspoon salt

¼ teaspoon freshly ground
    black pepper

Paprika, for garnish

1. In a food processor, pulse the garlic cloves until minced. Add the beans, 3 tablespoons of olive oil, lemon juice, tahini, oregano, salt, and pepper. Pulse until smooth.
2. Store the hummus in an airtight container for up to 3 days.
3. Just before serving, garnish the hummus with the remaining 1 tablespoon of olive oil and the paprika.

Makes 1½ cups. Prep time: 5 minutes.

Per serving (¼ cup):   Calories: 372   Fat: 14g   Saturated Fat: 2g   Protein: 18.7g
Carbohydrates: 46.2g   Fiber: 19.1g   Sodium: 125mg

Slow Cooker Applesauce

There are so many wonderful apples available now at the grocery store, especially when they are in season in the fall. For a tart applesauce, choose Granny Smith apples. For a sweeter apple-sauce, go for Golden Delicious apples. Other great selections include Jazz, Gala, Pink Lady, and Roma apples.

Cooking Tip: Unsweetened applesauce is often used in baking to replace oils and reduce the fat content of the product. This apple-sauce is a great contender for that, and should be pureed instead of left chunky if you'd like to use it for baking.

8 apples, peeled, cored, and cut into wedges

1 tablespoon lemon juice

1 tablespoon evaporated cane juice

1. Combine the apples, lemon juice, and cane juice in a 4- to 5-quart slow cooker.
2. Cover and cook on low for 6 hours. Stir occasionally.
3. Transfer the applesauce to a blender or food processor and pulse to desired consistency.

Makes 3 cups. Prep time: 10 minutes. Cooking time: 6 hours. Total time: 6 hours, 10 minutes.

. . . .

Per serving (¼ cup):   Calories: 65   Fat: 0g   Saturated Fat: 0g   Protein: 0g
Carbohydrates: 17.1g   Fiber: 2.9g

Chocolate-Almond Dip with Strawberries

For all you chocoholics, this is a great snack to calm your craving. Fiber from the strawberries and flaxseed, and protein from the almond butter, yogurt, and milk make it an ideal snack to keep you satisfied between meals. Flaxseed is packed with omega-3 fatty acids and lignans, which have powerful antioxidant properties.

Ingredient Tip: Did you know that bittersweet chocolate has been linked to good heart health? Be sure to choose at least 70% cacao content when selecting this tasty treat to get all of its health benefits.

½ cup all-natural
    almond butter
½ cup plain Greek yogurt
1 ounce 70% bittersweet
    chocolate, melted

¼ cup milk
2 tablespoons flaxseed
1 quart fresh strawberries

Stir together the almond butter, yogurt, chocolate, milk, and flaxseed. Serve with the strawberries.

Makes about 1¼ cups. Prep time: 10 minutes.

. . . .

Per serving (1 tablespoon):   Calories: 67   Fat: 4.6g   Saturated Fat: 0.9g   Protein: 2.3g
Carbohydrates: 4.8g   Fiber: 1.1g

8

Vegetarian
Dinners

Beet, Pear, and Mixed Greens Salad

Lettuce, along with being an amazing source of vitamins, minerals, and other nutrients, is high in protein; the beets help purify the liver and blood; and the pears are full of fiber, vitamins C and E, and potassium. All together they make this a delicious salad with many health benefits. With goat cheese and walnuts, it also happens to be very pretty!

1 pound beets (preferably the pink-and-white-striped chioggia variety), peeled and sliced paper thin

10 ounces mixed baby lettuces

⅓ cup Honey-Balsamic Vinaigrette (page 301)

4 ripe pears, halved and cored

4 ounces goat cheese, crumbled

½ cup chopped walnuts, toasted

1. In a large bowl, combine the beets, lettuce, and vinaigrette, and toss well to coat.
2. Divide the salad among four serving plates. Arrange two pear halves on each plate. Top each with the goat cheese and walnuts, and serve.

Serves 4. Prep time: 10 minutes.

. . . .

Per serving: Calories: 487   Fat: 28.3g   Saturated Fat: 8.7g   Protein: 15.4g
Carbohydrates: 50.2g   Fiber: 10.2g

Caprese Panini

Yummy, stringy mozzarella tops tomatoes and basil in these sandwiches based on the classic Italian caprese salad. *Insalata Caprese* means "salad of Capri," which is an island off of the southwestern coast of Italy. The colors represent the Italian flag. Just the smell and taste of fresh, in-season tomatoes and basil should be enough to transport you to the Italian seaside.

On-the-Go Tip: Panini are great take-along sandwiches. The press holds it all together and squeezes out the juices, making it easy to take wherever you're headed.

½ cup Basil Pesto (page 292)

8 slices 100% whole-
    grain bread

2 tomatoes, sliced

¼ cup fresh basil leaves

8 ounces fresh
    mozzarella, sliced

2 tablespoons avocado oil

1. Spread the pesto onto one side of each piece of bread. Top four slices evenly with the tomatoes, basil, and mozzarella. Top with the remaining four slices of bread.
2. Brush the avocado oil on a panini press or grill press. Add the sandwiches and close the press to cook. Alternatively, heat the oil in a large nonstick skillet over medium heat; add the sandwiches. Place a sheet of aluminum foil on top of the sandwiches and place a saucepan or plate over the foil filled with heavy canned goods.
3. Cook the sandwiches for 2 minutes. If using a skillet, turn and repeat the process until the cheese is melted and sandwiches are browned.
4. Serve immediately.

Serves 4. Prep time: 10 minutes. Cooking time: 5 minutes. Total time: 15 minutes.

. . . .

Per serving: Calories: 363   Fat: 14.2g   Saturated Fat: 6.3g   Protein: 25g
Carbohydrates: 34.9g   Fiber: 9.2g

Vegetarian Chili

When the weather outside is frightful, this chili will warm you from the inside-out. It provides 150% of your dietary fiber for the day and is high in potassium. Serve the chili with chunks of crusty 100% whole-grain bread for dipping.

Ingredient Variation: Swap out butternut squash for the sweet potato or other bean varieties for the pinto and kidney beans called for here.

2 tablespoons avocado oil

1 onion, chopped

1 green bell pepper, chopped

2 garlic cloves, minced

2 teaspoons ground cumin

1 teaspoon smoked paprika

½ teaspoon red pepper flakes

1 (14.5-ounce) can reduced-
    sodium vegetable broth

1 cup diced sweet potato

1 (28-ounce) can whole
    tomatoes, chopped

1 (15-ounce) can pinto beans,
    drained and rinsed

1 (15-ounce) can kidney beans,
    drained and rinsed

½ cup shredded sharp white
    Cheddar cheese

2 tablespoons chopped fresh
    cilantro leaves, for garnish

1. In a large Dutch oven over medium-high heat, heat the oil. Add the onion and bell pepper. Cook for 5 minutes or until tender.
2. Stir in the garlic, cumin, paprika, and red pepper flakes. Cook for 2 more minutes or until fragrant.
3. Add the vegetable broth, sweet potato, tomatoes, pinto beans, and kidney beans. Bring the mixture to a boil. Reduce the heat and simmer for 30 minutes or until the sweet potato is tender and the chili is thickened, stirring occasionally.
4. Serve the chili topped with cheese and garnished with cilantro.

Serves 4. Prep time: 5 minutes. Cooking time: 40 minutes. Total time: 45 minutes.

Per serving: Calories: 920   Fat: 9.5g   Saturated Fat: 3.9g   Protein: 56.1g
Carbohydrates: 156.5g   Fiber: 38.7g

Loaded Pinto Bean Nachos

This tasty take on traditional nachos can be served as a meal or as an appetizer for game-day gatherings. Double or triple the recipe to enjoy with family and friends.

Time-Saving Tip: Instead of making your own tortilla chips, buy 100% whole-grain chips at the store.

1 recipe Baked Tortilla Chips
    (page 133)

1 tablespoon avocado oil

2 teaspoons ground cumin

1 teaspoon chili powder

2 garlic cloves, minced

2 (15-ounce) cans pinto beans,
    drained and rinsed

½ cup reduced-sodium
    vegetable broth

1 cup crumbled feta cheese

1 cup Fresh Salsa (page 297)

1 avocado, diced

⅓ cup chopped fresh cilantro

1. Place the chips on a large serving platter.
2. In a medium saucepan over medium heat, heat the oil. Add the cumin, chili powder, and garlic. Cook for 1 minute or until the garlic is tender. Add the beans and broth. Cook for 5 minutes or until hot.
3. Remove the pan from the heat; mash the beans slightly with a potato masher. Spoon the bean mixture onto the chips.
4. Top with feta cheese, salsa, avocado, and cilantro.
5. Serve immediately.

Serves 6. Prep time: 10 minutes. Cooking time: 10 minutes. Total time: 20 minutes.

. . . .

Per serving: Calories: 812   Fat: 18.5g   Saturated Fat: 6.5g   Protein: 39.5g
Carbohydrates: 124.7g   Fiber: 27.9g

Grilled Mini Veggie Pizzas

Everyone loves pizza and this recipe can get the whole family involved. Make it a pizza night and let everyone top their own. Try other favorite toppings like mushrooms, uncured pepperoni, and fresh pineapple. This recipe is cooked on the grill so there's no need to mess up the kitchen!

Cooking Tip: Is the weather outside not ideal for grilling? Not to worry. This recipe can easily be made indoors. Either substitute a grill pan and cook the pizzas covered on the stove top, or bake the pizzas on a baking sheet at 425°F for 10 to 15 minutes.

4 (100%) whole-grain tortillas

1 cup Homemade Marinara Sauce (page 294)

2 cups sliced zucchini and yellow squash

½ cup sliced red onion

½ cup halved, pitted Kalamata olives

½ cup crumbled feta cheese

½ cup shredded white Cheddar cheese

1. Preheat the grill to medium heat.
2. Spread each tortilla with ¼ cup of marinara sauce; top evenly with the zucchini, yellow squash, onion, olives, and cheeses.
3. Cover the grill with the grill lid and cook for 2 to 3 minutes or until the tortillas are crisp and the cheese is melted.
4. Slice and serve.

Serves 4. Prep time: 15 minutes. Cooking time: 5 minutes. Total time: 20 minutes.

. . . .

Per serving: Calories: 275   Fat: 13.2g   Saturated Fat: 6.5g   Protein: 11.2g
Carbohydrates: 27.8g   Fiber: 5.1g

Eggplant Boats Stuffed with Quinoa, Tomato, and Feta

This recipe is a great one to get the kids involved. They will love these eggplant "boats" and they can help scoop out the eggplant halves, make the stuffing mixture, and load it into the boats.

Make-Ahead Tip: The eggplants can be stuffed and refrigerated the day before to help save on time during the week. Let them stand at room temperature for 30 minutes before baking.

2 small eggplants, trimmed and
    cut in half lengthwise

3 tablespoons avocado oil

1 teaspoon salt

1 teaspoon freshly ground
    black pepper

1 cup quinoa

2 garlic cloves, minced

1 tomato, chopped

1 (15-ounce) can cannellini
    beans, drained and rinsed

2 tablespoons balsamic vinegar

1 tablespoon chopped
    fresh oregano

6 ounces crumbled
    feta cheese

1. Preheat the oven to 350°F.
2. Line a rimmed baking sheet with aluminum foil.
3. Meanwhile, scoop the "meat" from the eggplants and place it in a medium bowl. Rub the insides of the eggplant boats with 1 tablespoon of oil, and sprinkle with ½ teaspoon each of salt and pepper.
4. Prepare the quinoa according to the package directions. Drain, and keep warm.
5. In a large nonstick skillet over medium-high heat, heat the oil. Add the garlic and the eggplant "meat." Cook for 7 to 8 minutes, stirring occasionally, until tender.

6. Combine the cooked eggplant mixture, quinoa, tomato, beans, vinegar, oregano, feta, and remaining ½ teaspoon each of salt and pepper.
7. Stuff each eggplant boat with the mixture and place them on the prepared baking sheet.
8. Bake for 45 minutes or until the eggplant is tender.
9. Serve hot.

Serves 4. Prep time: 20 minutes. Cooking time: 55 minutes.
Total time: 1 hour, 15 minutes.

. . . .

Per serving: Calories: 706   Fat: 14.5g   Saturated Fat: 7.1g   Protein: 40g
Carbohydrates: 109.8g   Fiber: 39.9g

Zucchini and Spinach Lasagna

This lasagna can be made ahead and frozen. Prepare all of the steps up through step 5, then cover it tightly with plastic wrap and foil. When you are ready to enjoy the lasagna, let it thaw overnight in the refrigerator. Bake as directed, adding an additional 15 to 20 minutes to the bake time. You can also refrigerate it for up to 2 days before baking it.

Perfect Pairing: Serve this classic dish with chopped romaine lettuce drizzled with Creamy Caesar Dressing (page 304).

12 (100%) whole-wheat lasagna noodles

16 ounces ricotta cheese

2 eggs

½ cup freshly grated Parmesan cheese

1 (10-ounce) package frozen chopped spinach, thawed and squeezed dry

2 tablespoons avocado oil

3 zucchini, sliced

1 (8-ounce) package sliced fresh mushrooms

2 garlic cloves, minced

½ teaspoon salt

½ teaspoon freshly ground black pepper

3 cups Homemade Marinara Sauce (page 294)

2 cups shredded mozzarella cheese

1. Preheat the oven to 375°F.
2. Cook the lasagna noodles according to the package directions; set aside.
3. In a medium bowl, stir together the ricotta cheese, eggs, Parmesan cheese, and spinach; set aside.
4. Heat the oil in a large nonstick skillet over medium heat; add the zucchini, mushrooms, garlic, salt, and pepper. Cook, stirring frequently, for 10 minutes or until the vegetables are tender. Remove the pan from the heat.

continued ▶

5. In a 13-by-9-inch baking dish, spread ¼ cup of marinara sauce. Top with 3 noodles. Top with ¾ cup of marinara sauce; top sauce with ⅓ of the ricotta mixture and ⅓ of the zucchini mixture.

6. Repeat the layers twice, ending with noodles. Spread the remaining marinara sauce over noodles. Top with the mozzarella cheese.

7. Bake 30 minutes or until bubbly. Let it stand for 10 minutes before serving.

Serves 8. Prep time: 15 minutes. Cooking time: 40 minutes.
Total time: 55 minutes (plus 10 minutes to cool).

. . . .

Per serving: Calories: 383   Fat: 18.6   Saturated Fat: 8g   Protein: 26.3g
Carbohydrates: 29.3g   Fiber: 5.8g

Mushroom Barley Risotto

In this recipe, risotto, the ultimate Italian comfort food, gets a makeover with barley in place of Arborio rice. The method is the same, producing a creamy mushroom-enhanced dish. The barley has more nutritional value than Arborio rice and adds a pleasing chewy texture and nutty flavor.

Cooking Tip: When cooking the mushrooms, be sure to brown them completely, allowing them to release all of their liquid. Doing so elevates the flavor of the risotto and prevents wateriness.

6 cups reduced-sodium vegetable broth

2 tablespoons avocado oil

3 garlic cloves, minced

½ cup chopped onion

1 pound portobello mushrooms, chopped

2 cups uncooked pearled barley

½ teaspoon dried thyme

½ teaspoon salt

½ teaspoon freshly ground black pepper

1 cup freshly grated Parmesan cheese

1. In a medium saucepan, heat the broth until very hot. Keep warm.
2. In a Dutch oven over medium heat, heat the oil. Add the garlic and onion; cook for 5 minutes or until the onion is tender. Add the mushrooms. Cook for 5 more minutes or until the mushrooms are tender and liquid has evaporated.
3. Stir in the barley. Cook for 1 minute or until toasted. Stir in the thyme and 1 cup of the hot broth. Cook for 3 minutes, or until nearly all the broth has evaporated.
4. Stir in the salt, pepper, and ¾ cup of broth. Cook, stirring constantly, until the broth is nearly all evaporated. Continue adding more broth ½ cup at a time, until the barley is tender and the risotto is creamy, 18 to 20 minutes. Stir in the cheese just before serving.

Serves 4. Prep time: 10 minutes. Cooking time: 35 minutes. Total time: 45 minutes.

. . . .

Per serving: Calories: 524   Fat: 11.4g   Saturated Fat: 5.3g   Protein: 31.1g
Carbohydrates: 78.5g   Fiber: 18.4g

Garden Vegetable Pasta Sauce with Parmesan Spaghetti Squash

If you are new to spaghetti squash, you are going to love it. After the squash is cooked, the flesh resembles long spaghetti-like strands. It's a healthy and tasty substitute for pasta and adds extra fiber to your diet.

Time-Saving Tip: This recipe calls for making homemade marinara sauce, but in a pinch you can buy prepared marinara sauce to lessen the prep time. Look for organic sauce with no added sugar or sodium.

1 spaghetti squash

3 tablespoons avocado oil

½ teaspoon salt

½ teaspoon freshly ground black pepper

2 zucchini, sliced

2 carrots, peeled and chopped

1 onion, chopped

8 ounces sliced fresh mushrooms

2 cups Homemade Marinara Sauce (page 294)

1 cup freshly grated Parmesan cheese

1. Preheat the oven to 450°F. Line a rimmed baking sheet with aluminum foil.
2. Cut the spaghetti squash in half, and scrape out the seeds. Drizzle the inside with 2 tablespoons of oil, and sprinkle with the salt and pepper.
3. Place the spaghetti squash flesh-side down on prepared baking sheet.
4. Bake for 30 to 40 minutes or until tender.
5. Meanwhile, in a large saucepan over medium-high heat, add the zucchini, carrots, onion, and mushrooms. Cook, stirring frequently, for 15 minutes, or until the vegetables are tender.

6. Stir in the marinara sauce. Cook for 5 more minutes or until it is thoroughly heated.
7. Remove the squash from the oven and use a fork to scrape the flesh into large strands. Transfer the squash to a serving bowl. Stir in the Parmesan cheese and top with the marinara-vegetable mixture. Serve.

Serves 4. Prep time: 15 minutes. Cooking time: 30 minutes. Total time: 45 minutes.

. . . .

Per serving: Calories: 300   Fat: 15.9g   Saturated Fat: 5.6g   Protein: 15g
Carbohydrates: 30.4g   Fiber: 4.5g

Grilled Portobello Burgers with Sweet Potato Fries

Caramelized balsamic onions and blue cheese perched atop a savory, tender mushroom burger could be considered the ultimate meal. The use of balsamic vinegar helps speed up the caramelizing process, and the tangy cheese is the perfect balance to the sweet-tart vinegar. Served with homemade sweet potato fries, this is a dinner the whole family is sure to enjoy.

Cooking Tip: For the crispiest sweet potato fries, try turning them once or twice during baking. Wait until the sides touching the bottom are nice and brown before turning.

For the burgers:

2 tablespoons avocado oil

2 onions, thinly sliced

3 tablespoons balsamic vinegar

4 (4-inch) portobello
    mushroom caps, cleaned
    and stems removed

½ teaspoon salt

½ teaspoon freshly ground
    black pepper

½ cup crumbled blue cheese

4 (100%) whole-wheat
    hamburger buns, lightly
    toasted

¼ cup Homemade Mayonnaise
    (page 288)

1 cup fresh baby spinach

For the sweet potato fries:

2 tablespoons avocado oil, plus
    additional for greasing

2 large sweet potatoes, cut into
    ¼-inch-thick wedges

½ teaspoon salt

½ teaspoon freshly ground
    black pepper

1 teaspoon smoked paprika

To make the burgers:

1. Preheat the grill to high heat.
2. In a large skillet over medium heat, heat 1 tablespoon of oil. Add the onions and cook, covered, for 10 minutes or until they are very soft. Add 1 tablespoon of vinegar. Cook for about 5 minutes, stirring occasionally, until the onions are caramelized.

continued ▶

3. In a small bowl, whisk together the remaining 1 tablespoon of oil and remaining 2 tablespoons of vinegar. Brush the mixture evenly on both sides of the mushroom caps. Sprinkle the mushrooms with salt and pepper. Grill, covered with the grill lid, for 8 minutes or until the mushrooms are tender, turning occasionally. Remove the mushrooms from grill to a platter and sprinkle them evenly with the blue cheese.
4. Spread 1 tablespoon of mayonnaise on each of the four bottom bun halves. Top each with one portobello cap, ¼ of the onions, and ¼ cup of spinach. Top with bun tops.

To make the sweet potato fries:
1. Preheat the oven to 425°F.
2. Coat a rimmed baking sheet with the oil.
3. In a large bowl, toss together the sweet potatoes, 2 tablespoons of oil, salt, pepper, and paprika. Spread the potatoes on the prepared baking sheet. Bake for 15 to 20 minutes, turning occasionally, until the sweet potatoes are browned and tender.
4. Serve hot alongside the burgers.

Serves 4. Prep time: 10 minutes. Cooking time: 25 minutes. Total time: 35 minutes.

. . . .

Per serving: Calories: 402   Fat: 13.6g   Saturated Fat: 4.6g   Protein: 10.2g
Carbohydrates: 62g   Fiber: 10g

Summer Panzanella

A staple in Italian cuisine, this salad was originally created to make use of stale, day-old bread. To create the dry bread, the recipe calls for toasting it, but you may also buy the bread a day in advance and let the cubes dry out overnight, turning once, on a baking sheet in a cold oven.

Ingredient Tip: If it's summertime, you may see colorful heirloom tomatoes at the grocery store or at your local farmers' market. Take advantage of the season and snatch them up. Not only will they make a gorgeous salad, but they also deliver the ultimate in tomato flavor.

4 tomatoes, coarsely chopped

1 cucumber, coarsely chopped

½ cup thinly sliced red onion

½ cup pitted Kalamata olives

½ cup fresh basil leaves

8 ounces 100% whole-wheat bread, cut into 1-inch cubes and toasted

8 ounces fresh mozzarella, cut into small pieces

⅓ cup Honey-Balsamic Vinaigrette (page 301)

1. In a large bowl, combine the tomatoes, cucumber, onion, olives, basil, bread, and mozzarella.
2. Pour the dressing over the salad; toss well to coat. Serve immediately.

Serves 4. Prep time: 15 minutes.

Per serving: Calories: 362   Fat: 14.2g   Saturated Fat: 6.8g   Protein: 25.4g
Carbohydrates: 35.5g   Fiber: 6.7g

Sweet Potato and Lentil Tagine

Tagines are stews native to North Africa which are made with certain spice blends for seasoning. This one uses garam masala, a spice blend hailing from India. Every bottled garam masala blend is different, but most include a mixture of ground turmeric, black pepper, cloves, cinnamon, cumin, and cardamom. The term tagine is used for both the stew and for the lidded ceramic pot it is traditionally cooked in.

Make-Ahead Tip: This hearty stew improves in flavor over time and gets thicker. It's a great make-ahead dish, so try doubling it to have as leftovers during the week. In addition to serving it over the traditional couscous, you could try serving it with brown basmati rice.

For the tagine:

2 tablespoons coconut oil

3 cups chopped cabbage

12 ounces sweet potato, peeled and cubed

1 onion, chopped

½ cup dried brown lentils

¼ cup chopped dried apricots

1 tablespoon grated fresh ginger

1 tablespoon garam masala

½ teaspoon salt

½ teaspoon freshly ground black pepper

Juice and zest of ½ lemon

2 (14.5-ounce) cans reduced-sodium vegetable broth

1 (14.5-ounce) can diced tomatoes, undrained

For the couscous:

1 (14.5-ounce) can reduced-sodium vegetable broth

½ cup water

1½ cups 100% whole-wheat couscous

¼ cup chopped fresh parsley

To make the tagine:

1. In a large Dutch oven over medium heat, heat the oil. Add the cabbage, sweet potato, onion, lentils, apricots, and ginger. Cook for 3 minutes, stirring frequently.

2. Stir in the garam masala, salt, and pepper. Cook for 1 minute, stirring frequently.
3. Add the lemon juice and zest, broth, and tomatoes; bring to a boil.
4. Reduce the heat and simmer, uncovered, for 40 minutes or until the lentils are tender.

To make the couscous:
1. In a medium saucepan, bring the broth and water to a boil.
2. Add the couscous. Return the liquid to a simmer, cover, and then remove the saucepan from the heat.
3. Let stand, covered, for 5 minutes. Fluff with a fork and stir in the parsley.
4. Serve the tangine over a bed of couscous.

Serves 6. Prep time: 10 minutes. Cooking time: 45 minutes. Total time: 55 minutes.

. . . .

Per serving: Calories: 907   Fat: 7.6g   Saturated Fat: 4.5g   Protein: 38g
Carbohydrates: 168.4g   Fiber: 17g

Roasted Butternut Squash and Israeli Couscous Pilaf

Israeli couscous is toasted pasta that is shaped like a ball. It is not that much different than couscous, which is also made from semolina flour, except a little heartier and it does not clump together when cooked. The mint, olives, and lemon are standards of Middle Eastern cooking and make this a lively dish.

Ingredient Tip: Sometimes butternut squash can be challenging to cut. To make things easier on you, try pricking the squash a few times with a fork. Then, microwave it on high for 1 to 2 minutes to soften up the squash.

3 tablespoons coconut oil, plus additional for greasing

2 pounds butternut squash, peeled and cut into chunks

1 teaspoon salt

1 teaspoon freshly ground black pepper

½ teaspoon ground cumin

¼ teaspoon cayenne pepper

1½ cups 100% whole-wheat pearled couscous (Israeli couscous)

2 garlic cloves, minced

2 cups water

½ cup Kalamata olives, halved

¼ cup chopped fresh mint

¼ cup sliced almonds, toasted

1 teaspoon grated lemon zest

1. Preheat the oven to 475°F.
2. Coat a rimmed baking sheet with oil.
3. Combine the butternut squash, 2 tablespoons of coconut oil, ½ teaspoon each of salt and pepper, cumin, and cayenne pepper on the baking sheet.
4. Bake for 20 minutes or until tender and golden brown.
5. Meanwhile, in a medium saucepan, heat the remaining 1 tablespoon of coconut oil over medium-high heat. Add the couscous and garlic; sauté for 1 minute.

continued ▶

6. Stir in the water, the remaining ½ teaspoon of salt, and ½ teaspoon of pepper. Bring to a boil; reduce the heat, and simmer for 12 minutes or until the liquid is absorbed.
7. Remove the saucepan from the heat and stir in the olives, mint, almonds, lemon zest, and roasted butternut squash. Toss well to combine.
8. Serve immediately.

Serves 4. Prep time: 15 minutes. Cooking time: 20 minutes. Total time: 35 minutes.

. . . .

Per serving: Calories: 447   Fat: 16.5g   Saturated Fat: 9.4g   Protein: 12.1g
Carbohydrates: 75.6g   Fiber: 13.6g

Creole Red Beans and Rice

Vegan
Gluten-Free

This classic Louisiana dish will have everyone in the family asking for seconds. If you use fresh herbs, triple the amount of fresh to herbs (1 teaspoon dried = 1 tablespoon fresh).

Ingredient Tip: This recipe calls for time-saving pre-chopped onion, celery, and bell pepper—also known as "trinity mix" in Creole cooking. It's often in the supermarket around Thanksgiving and other holidays. Two cups of a mix of these vegetables will work perfectly.

1½ cups uncooked brown rice

2 tablespoons coconut oil

1 (8-ounce) package pre-chopped onion, celery, and bell pepper

3 garlic cloves, minced

2 (15-ounce) cans red beans, drained and rinsed

1 (14.5-ounce) can diced tomatoes

1 (14.5-ounce) can reduced-sodium vegetable broth

1 teaspoon dried thyme

1 teaspoon dried oregano

1 teaspoon smoked paprika

¾ teaspoon salt

½ teaspoon freshly ground black pepper

½ teaspoon cayenne pepper

Hot sauce (optional)

1. Prepare rice according to the package directions; keep warm.
2. In a large Dutch oven over medium-high heat, heat the oil. Add the onion, celery, and bell pepper mix. Cook for 5 minutes or until the vegetables are tender. Add the garlic; cook for 2 more minutes.
3. Mash one can of beans. Add the mashed beans, remaining can of beans, tomatoes, broth, thyme, oregano, paprika, salt, pepper, and cayenne pepper to the Dutch oven.
4. Bring to a boil. Reduce heat, and simmer, covered, for 30 minutes or until the mixture is very hot and slightly thickened. Serve the Creole red beans over rice with hot sauce (if using).

Serves 4. Prep time: 10 minutes. Cooking time: 1 hour. Total time: 1 hour, 10 minutes.

....

Per serving: Calories: 1,089 Fat: 11.9g Saturated Fat: 6.8g Protein: 56.6g
Carbohydrates: 194.1g Fiber: 38g

Marinated Tofu and Vegetable Kabobs

Fire up the grill and enjoy these tasty tofu skewers without heating up the kitchen. If it's cold or rainy outside, you can use an indoor grill pan instead. To drain the tofu before cutting it, see the Sweet Chili-Tofu and Sugar Snap Stir-Fry recipe's Cooking Tip on page 182.

Cooking Tip: Soak the wooden skewers in water for 30 minutes before threading them with ingredients to prevent them from burning on the grill.

1 pound firm tofu, drained
    and pressed dry
2 red bell peppers, cut into
    1-inch pieces
1 red onion, cut into wedges
8 ounces small whole
    mushrooms
2 cups fresh pineapple chunks
⅓ cup avocado oil

⅓ cup lemon juice
¼ cup water
¼ cup Dijon mustard
2 tablespoons honey
2 garlic cloves, minced
1 tablespoon grated
    fresh ginger
2 tablespoons chopped
    fresh cilantro

1. Cut the tofu into 1-inch cubes. Thread the tofu, bell peppers, onion, mushrooms, and pineapple alternately onto 8 (10-inch) wooden skewers.
2. Place the skewers in a baking dish.
3. Whisk together the oil, lemon juice, water, mustard, honey, garlic, ginger, and cilantro. Pour the mixture over the skewers. Cover and refrigerate the kebabs for 2 hours.
4. Preheat the grill to medium heat.
5. Grill the kabobs for 10 minutes, turning occasionally, until the vegetables are tender.
6. Serve the kebabs on the skewer.

Serves 4. Prep time: 15 minutes. Cooking time: 10 minutes.
Total time: 25 minutes (plus 2 hours to marinate).

....

Per serving: Calories: 238   Fat: 8.3g   Saturated Fat: 1.7g   Protein: 13g
Carbohydrates: 31.3g   Fiber: 6.2g

Vegetable Fried Rice

Fried rice is a delicious, quick meal for weeknights. This version has nutritious vegetables and cashews for a tasty crunch. Try adding seared tofu to this classic Chinese dish for additional protein. Or, if you aren't vegetarian, stir in cooked chicken, cooked pork, or steamed shrimp.

Time-Saving Tip: To make preparing this dish super fast, use leftover rice from a meal earlier in the week. It will cut down the total time to 20 minutes!

1½ cups uncooked brown rice

2 tablespoons coconut oil

3 eggs, lightly beaten

3 green onions, cut into 1-inch pieces

3 cups frozen mixed vegetables, thawed

1 red bell pepper, cut into strips

2 garlic cloves, minced

1 teaspoon grated fresh ginger

2 tablespoons brown rice vinegar

3 tablespoons tamari or coconut aminos

1 tablespoon dark sesame oil

1 cup unsalted cashews

1. Cook the rice according to the package directions and set aside.
2. In a large nonstick skillet over medium-high heat, heat 1 tablespoon of coconut oil. Add the eggs, and cook for 1 minute, or until done, stirring with a spatula to scramble. Remove the egg from the pan, and keep warm.
3. Add the remaining 1 tablespoon of coconut oil to the pan. Add the green onions, frozen vegetables, bell pepper, garlic, and ginger. Sauté for 5 minutes or until the vegetables are tender.
4. In a small bowl, whisk together the vinegar, tamari, and sesame oil. Add the cooked rice to pan. Stir in egg and vinegar mixture. Cook for 30 seconds or until mixture is hot, stirring constantly. Top each serving with cashews.

Serves 4. Prep time: 10 minutes. Cooking time: 1 hour. Total time: 1 hour, 10 minutes.

....

Per serving: Calories: 709   Fat: 31.6g   Saturated Fat: 11g   Protein: 20.7g
Carbohydrates: 87.8g   Fiber: 10.6g

Curried Chickpeas with Spinach and Brown Rice

Curry powder is a blend of several spices, and the spice combination can vary by brand. Most curry powders include a mixture of spices like cumin, turmeric, coriander, and fenugreek. You can also find versions with ground ginger, cloves, nutmeg, and mustard. Whichever you prefer, it's a great spice mix to have on hand to add a boost to a dish.

1 cup uncooked brown rice

2 tablespoons coconut oil

1 cup chopped red onion

2 garlic cloves, minced

1 tablespoon grated
    fresh ginger

2 tablespoons curry powder

1 (10-ounce) bag fresh
    baby spinach

1 (14.5-ounce) can stewed
    tomatoes, drained

1 (14.5-ounce) can reduced-
    sodium vegetable broth

2 (15.5-ounce) cans chickpeas,
    drained and rinsed

4 sprigs fresh basil leaves,
    for garnish

1. Cook the rice according to the package instructions.
2. In a large skillet over medium heat, heat the coconut oil; add the onion, garlic, and ginger and sauté for 5 minutes or until the onion is tender.
3. Stir in the curry powder and cook for 1 more minute.
4. Add the spinach, tomatoes, and vegetable broth. Cook for 5 minutes or until the spinach is wilted.
5. Add the chickpeas. Cook for 10 more minutes or until the sauce is thickened.
6. Serve the chickpea mixture in bowls, garnished with the basil, with the rice alongside for spooning into the individual bowls.

Serves 4. Prep time: 5 minutes. Cooking time: 40 minutes. Total time: 45 minutes.

....

Per serving: Calories: 1,039 Fat: 21.8g Saturated Fat: 7.7g Protein: 48g
Carbohydrates: 170.3g Fiber: 41.1g

Sweet Chili-Tofu and Sugar Snap Stir-Fry

The sauce is the real standout in this Asian-inspired dish. On its own, tofu doesn't have much flavor but it is known for absorbing the flavors around it. A homemade marinade gives the tofu the sweet-tangy tastes of pineapple juice, ginger, and honey, and chili hot sauce adds the heat.

Cooking Tip: To drain the tofu well, place it on a rimmed baking sheet and cover it with paper towels. Place a heavy saucepan over the top loaded with canned goods. Let it stand for 5 to 10 minutes to release any extra moisture. Transfer the drained tofu to a cutting board to cut it into cubes. The drained tofu will cut easily, brown nicely, and will absorb the tasty marinade.

8 ounces brown rice noodles

1 tablespoon coconut oil

1 (12.3-ounce) package firm tofu, drained and cubed

2 (12-ounce) packages frozen sugar snap peas, broccoli, carrots, and water chestnuts, thawed

¾ cup Asian Marinade (page 305)

1 tablespoon sambal oelek chili hot sauce

1 tablespoon arrowroot powder

1. Prepare the noodles according to the package directions; drain, and keep warm.
2. In a large skillet over medium-high heat, heat the oil. Add the tofu, and cook for 4 to 5 minutes or until the tofu is lightly browned, stirring often. Remove the tofu, and keep warm.
3. Add the sugar snap peas, broccoli, carrots, and water chestnuts to the skillet. Cover and steam for 3 minutes or until the vegetables are hot.

4. In a small bowl, whisk together the marinade, hot sauce, and arrowroot powder. Add the mixture to the skillet with tofu. Cook for 3 minutes or until the sauce is thickened. Serve the vegetable and tofu mixture over the noodles.

Serves 4. Prep time: 15 minutes. Cooking time: 30 minutes. Total time: 45 minutes.

....

Per serving: Calories: 452   Fat: 9.5g   Saturated Fat: 4.2g   Protein: 16.6g
Carbohydrates: 76.7g   Fiber: 7.1g

Vietnamese Tofu Lettuce Wraps

Fish sauce is a potent condiment common to Vietnamese cuisine. If you are following a strict vegetarian diet, you may substitute brown rice vinegar for the fish sauce or omit it completely. For instructions on draining the tofu, see the Cooking Tip (page 182).

1 pound extra-firm tofu, drained

½ cup lime juice

¼ cup honey

3 garlic cloves, minced

2 tablespoons fish sauce (optional)

2 tablespoons tamari or coconut aminos

1 tablespoon grated fresh ginger

1 teaspoon sambal oelek chili hot sauce

1 tablespoon coconut oil

1 head Boston lettuce, leaves separated

½ cup fresh cilantro leaves

¼ cup fresh mint leaves

¼ cup chopped dry-roasted peanuts

1 carrot, peeled and grated

½ cucumber, thinly sliced

1. Place the tofu in a shallow baking dish. In a medium bowl, whisk together the lime juice, honey, garlic, fish sauce (if using), tamari, ginger, and hot sauce. Pour the marinade over the tofu. Cover and let it stand for 30 minutes. Remove the tofu from the dish, reserving the marinade.
2. Heat a large nonstick skillet over medium-high heat; add the coconut oil. Brown the tofu slices for 3 minutes on each side.
3. Place one tofu slice in the center of each lettuce leaf. Top with cilantro, mint, peanuts, carrot, and cucumber. Drizzle with the reserved marinade, and roll up.

Serves 4. Prep time: 10 minutes. Cooking time: 10 minutes.
Total time: 20 minutes (plus 30 minutes to drain and 30 minutes to marinate).

. . . .

Per serving: Calories: 404   Fat: 24.6g   Saturated Fat: 5.6g   Protein: 21.3g
Carbohydrates: 35.1g   Fiber: 4.8g

Falafel Pitas with Tzatziki Sauce

Falafel, a staple of Middle Eastern cuisine, are chickpea patties mixed with spices served in pita bread. They are traditionally deep fried, but in this recipe, the falafel are sautéed in healthy avocado oil and the pita is packed with spinach, tomato, and cool cucumber and yogurt tzatziki sauce.

Make-Ahead Tip: To help save time, make the chickpea patties in advance up through step 2. Keep them covered in the refrigerator for up to 2 days until you are ready to cook them.

1 (15.5-ounce) can chickpeas, drained and rinsed

1 garlic clove

¼ cup chopped red onion

¼ cup chopped fresh cilantro

1 egg

¼ cup 100% whole-wheat Panko bread crumbs

2 teaspoons ground cumin

¼ teaspoon salt

¼ teaspoon freshly ground black pepper

¼ cup 100% whole-wheat pastry flour

3 tablespoons avocado oil

2 (100%) whole-wheat pitas, halved and split

2 cups fresh baby spinach

2 tomatoes, sliced

1 cup Tzatziki Sauce (page 295)

1. In a food processor, combine the chickpeas, garlic, onion, and cilantro; pulse until it is chopped. Add the egg, bread crumbs, cumin, salt, and pepper. Pulse until a paste forms.
2. Shape the mixture into 8 patties. Dredge the patties in the flour.
3. In a large nonstick skillet over medium heat, heat the oil. Cook the patties, for 2 to 3 minutes on each side or until browned and done.
4. Place 2 patties in each pita half. Top with spinach, tomatoes, and tzatziki sauce.

Serves 4. Prep time: 10 minutes. Cooking time: 10 minutes. Total time: 20 minutes.

....

Per serving: Calories: 576   Fat: 11.5g   Saturated Fat: 2.4g   Protein: 28g
Carbohydrates: 95.3g   Fiber: 24g

9

Fish and
Seafood Dinners

Coconut Shrimp with Sesame Green Beans

Finally! Restaurant-style supremely delicious coconut shrimp you can make at home and that are good for you! The egg white foam creates the perfect dipping substance and makes the coconut crust extra crispy.

Cooking Tip: These shrimp can also be baked instead of pan-fried. While a 400°F oven preheats, place a coconut oil–coated baking sheet in the oven. When the pan is hot, place the coated shrimp on the pan. Bake for 2 minutes, and then turn shrimp and bake for 3 minutes more.

For the shrimp:

1½ pounds peeled and deveined large shrimp

½ teaspoon salt

¼ cup 100% whole-wheat pastry flour

2 cups unsweetened shredded coconut

3 egg whites

3 tablespoons coconut oil

½ cup Honey-Mustard Dipping Sauce (page 289)

1 teaspoon curry powder

For the green beans:

1 (16-ounce) package frozen green beans

1 tablespoon dark (toasted) sesame oil

1 tablespoon tamari or coconut aminos

1 tablespoon toasted sesame seeds

To make the shrimp:

1. Sprinkle the shrimp with salt. Place the flour in a shallow dish; place the coconut in a separate shallow dish.
2. In a medium bowl, beat the egg whites until soft peaks form. Dredge the shrimp in the flour, shaking off the excess. Dip the shrimp in the egg whites, and then in coconut, pressing to adhere.

3. Heat the oil in a large nonstick skillet over medium-high heat. Add the shrimp to the skillet and cook for 2 to 3 minutes on each side or until they are browned and crispy.
4. In a small bowl, stir together the dipping sauce and curry powder.

To make the green beans:

1. Place the green beans in a steamer basket in a medium saucepan over simmering water. Cover and cook for 5 minutes or until crisp-tender.
2. Transfer the green beans to a serving bowl. Add the sesame oil, tamari, and sesame seeds, tossing well to coat.
3. Serve the shrimp hot with the green beans, and pass the dipping sauce for the shrimp.

Serves 4. Prep time: 20 minutes. Cooking time: 10 minutes. Total time: 30 minutes.

. . . .

Per serving: Calories: 513   Fat: 30g   Saturated Fat: 21.4g   Protein: 34.2g
Carbohydrates: 29.1g   Fiber: 7.7g

Baked Lemon-Dill Snapper Packets

These parchment paper packets make this an elegant and succulent one-dish meal that, while impressive, is easy to prepare. Cut the red bell pepper strips to the same size as the green beans so they'll cook up evenly.

Perfect Pairing: Serve these baked fish and vegetable parcels with steamed brown rice.

2 red bell peppers, thinly sliced
1 cup green beans, trimmed
1 cup yellow wax beans, trimmed
1 cup peas
2 garlic cloves, sliced
4 skinless red snapper fillets
1 teaspoon salt

1 teaspoon freshly ground
    black pepper
2 lemons
8 dill sprigs
2 tablespoons avocado oil
1 tablespoon Dijon mustard

1. Preheat the oven to 400°F.
2. Lay four (24-inch) pieces of parchment paper on the countertop.
3. Divide the bell peppers, green beans, yellow wax beans, peas, and garlic evenly among the four pieces of parchment, placing the vegetables in the center of each square.
4. Place a snapper fillet on top of each bed of vegetables; sprinkle each with salt and pepper.
5. Slice 1 lemon and place the slices on top of each snapper with 2 dill sprigs.
6. In a small bowl, whisk together the juice from the remaining lemon, avocado oil, and Dijon mustard. Drizzle the mixture over the fish.
7. Lift the sides of the parchment over the ingredients and fold them together to enclose the fish and vegetables in a bag-like packet. Seal the packets by making several small overlapping folds along the edge.

continued ▶

8. Transfer the packets to a large rimmed baking sheet. Bake for 15 to 18 minutes, or until the packets have puffed and the fish is cooked.

9. Transfer the packets to serving plates and open them. Fold down the sides of the parchment to reveal the fish and vegetables inside and serve immediately.

Serves 4. Prep time: 25 minutes. Cooking time: 15 minutes. Total time: 40 minutes.

. . . .

Per serving: Calories: 173   Fat: 2.7g   Saturated Fat: 0g   Protein: 24.8g
Carbohydrates: 14.4g   Fiber: 5.5g

Spice-Rubbed Salmon with Citrus Salsa and Steamed Green Beans

Gluten-Free
Dairy-Free

This simple spice-rubbed salmon gets its flavor from cumin and smoked paprika. It's topped off with a sweet and tart salsa, a hint of spice from jalapeño, and fresh cilantro. For a variation, make salmon tacos with 100% whole-grain tortillas, shredded cabbage, and salsa.

Cooking Tip: This recipe asks you to peel and section the oranges and grapefruit. With a paring knife, carefully remove the peel and bitter white pith from the fruit. Then, while holding the fruit over a bowl to collect the juice, follow the natural sections of the fruit with the knife, cutting a wedge to release the fruit. This step can easily be done in advance.

4 skinless salmon fillets

1 teaspoon ground cumin

1 teaspoon smoked paprika

1 teaspoon salt

1 teaspoon freshly ground black pepper

½ pound fresh green beans, trimmed

2 oranges, peeled and sectioned

1 ruby red grapefruit, peeled and sectioned

1 jalapeño pepper, minced

Juice and zest of 1 lime

¼ cup extra-virgin olive oil

3 tablespoons chopped fresh cilantro

1. Preheat the grill to medium-high heat.
2. Rub the salmon fillets evenly with cumin, paprika, and ½ teaspoon each of salt and pepper. Place the green beans on a large sheet of aluminum foil; sprinkle evenly with ¼ teaspoon each of salt and pepper. Fold the aluminum foil to create a packet.
3. Grill the salmon for 3 to 4 minutes on each side or until done. Grill the green beans for 10 minutes or until crisp-tender.

continued ▶

4. Chop the oranges and grapefruit and place them in a medium bowl. Stir in the remaining ¼ teaspoon each of salt and pepper, jalapeño pepper, lime juice and zest, olive oil, and cilantro.
5. Spoon the salsa over the salmon. Serve the salmon with the green beans on the side.

Serves 4. Prep time: 15 minutes. Cooking time: 10 minutes. Total time: 25 minutes.

. . . .

Per serving: Calories: 343 Fat: 14.6g Saturated Fat: 1.9g Protein: 38.6g
Carbohydrates: 21g Fiber: 5.6g

Sesame Tuna with Edamame Salad

Gluten-Free
Dairy-Free

For a lively touch that doesn't change the flavor, top the tuna with a mixture of black and white sesame seeds. You can find the already mixed seeds, called *gomasio* in Japanese, in the Asian food section of the grocery store. Edamame is nothing other than fresh soy beans. It is rich in nutrients such as folates, manganese, and vitamin K as well as protein and dietary fiber.

On-the-Go Tip: This makes a great take-away lunch. Slice the tuna and mix it with the edamame salad. Store it in the refrigerator and take it for lunch.

For the tuna:
½ cup Asian Marinade
    (page 305)
4 (6-ounce) tuna steaks
¼ cup sesame seeds
1 teaspoon arrowroot powder
2 tablespoons coconut oil

For the edamame salad:
3 cups frozen shelled
    edamame, thawed
1 cup shredded red cabbage
1 red bell pepper, finely chopped
1 carrot, peeled and shredded
¼ cup chopped fresh cilantro
3 tablespoons freshly squeezed
    orange juice (1 orange)
1 tablespoon dark sesame oil
1 tablespoon tamari or
    coconut aminos

To make the tuna:

1. Place 2 tablespoons of the marinade in shallow dish; dip the tuna in the marinade.
2. Place the sesame seeds in a separate shallow dish; dip the tuna in the sesame seeds.
3. In a small bowl, whisk together the remaining 6 tablespoons of marinade and arrowroot powder; set aside.

continued ▶

4. Heat the oil in a large nonstick skillet over medium-high heat. Sear the tuna for 1 to 2 minutes on each side or to the desired doneness. Remove the cooked tuna from the pan.
5. Add the marinade mixture to skillet. Cook for 1 to 2 minutes or until the sauce is thickened. Serve with the tuna.

To make the edamame salad:

1. In a large bowl, stir together edamame, cabbage, bell pepper, carrot, and cilantro.
2. In a small bowl, whisk together the orange juice, sesame oil, and tamari. Pour the dressing over the salad, tossing to coat.
3. Serve the salad alongside the tuna and sauce.

Serves 4. Prep time: 15 minutes. Cooking time: 5 minutes. Total time: 20 minutes.

. . . .

Per serving: Calories: 674   Fat: 30g   Saturated Fat: 9.8g   Protein: 65.7g
Carbohydrates: 32g   Fiber: 8.5g

Shrimp Succotash

Succotash comes from eastern Native Americans who relied on crops in season. The fresh corn, tomatoes, and basil all epitomize summer. The smoky bacon and sweet shrimp round out this one-dish meal perfectly.

On-the-Go Tip: Have leftovers? This dish makes the perfect lunch and is great cold or at room temperature. Store it in an airtight container in the refrigerator for up to 2 days.

2 slices natural, uncured bacon

1½ pounds peeled and
   deveined large shrimp

¾ teaspoon salt

½ teaspoon freshly ground
   black pepper

2 garlic cloves, minced

2 cups frozen lima beans, thawed

1 cup fresh corn kernels
   (about 2 ears)

1 (14.5-ounce) can reduced-
   sodium chicken broth

2 cups chopped tomatoes

¼ cup fresh basil leaves

1. In a large Dutch oven over medium heat, cook the bacon until crisp, about 10 minutes. Remove the bacon to a paper towel–lined plate to drain. Crumble the bacon.
2. Sprinkle the shrimp with ½ teaspoon each of salt and pepper. Add the shrimp to the bacon drippings in the skillet, and cook, stirring occasionally, for 4 to 5 minutes, until pink and just cooked through. Remove the shrimp from the pan, and keep warm.
3. Add the garlic to pan. Cook for 1 minute or until tender. Add the lima beans, corn, chicken broth, and remaining ¼ teaspoon of salt. Increase the heat to medium-high, and bring just to a simmer. Reduce the heat and simmer, uncovered, for 10 minutes or until the vegetables are tender.
4. Stir in the shrimp, tomatoes, bacon, and basil. Cook for 1 minute or until thoroughly heated through. Serve hot.

Serves 4. Prep time: 10 minutes. Cooking time: 25 minutes. Total time: 35 minutes.

. . . .

Per serving: Calories: 286   Fat: 4.5g   Saturated Fat: 0.9g   Protein: 37.3g
Carbohydrates: 26.8g   Fiber: 5.7g

Tuna Niçoise Salad

Gluten-Free
Dairy-Free

This traditional, composed French tuna and fresh vegetable salad includes elements that can be made ahead. Try cooking the potatoes, green beans, and hard-boiled eggs eggs a day or two in advance or make the vinaigrette the day before to help save time with dinner prep.

Cooking Tip: This recipe calls for hard-boiled eggs. Place the eggs in a saucepan with water to cover and bring to a boil. Remove the pan from the heat and let it stand for 15 minutes. Drain.

½ pound new potatoes, halved

¼ pound fresh green
  beans, trimmed

1 pound tuna steaks

½ teaspoon salt

½ teaspoon freshly ground
  black pepper

1 tablespoon avocado oil

4 cups chopped romaine lettuce

2 tomatoes, cut into wedges

½ cup Kalamata olives

½ cup Mustard-Thyme
  Vinaigrette (page 303)

4 hard-boiled eggs, peeled
  and quartered

1. In a medium pot, add the potatoes, cover them with water, and bring to a boil. Cook for 15 minutes or until the potatoes are tender. Add the green beans during the last 5 minutes of cooking.
2. Drain the potatoes and green beans; rinse with cold water to cool.
3. Sprinkle the tuna with salt and pepper. Heat the oil in a large nonstick skillet over medium-high heat. Sear the tuna for 1 to 2 minutes on each side or to the desired doneness. Set aside.
4. On four individual serving plates, lay down a bed of chopped romaine and then group the potatoes, green beans, tomatoes, and olives on top. Slice the seared tuna and divide it evenly among the plates.
5. Pour the vinaigrette over the salad to dress. Place 4 egg quarters on each plate.

Serves 4. Prep time: 15 minutes. Cooking time: 15 minutes. Total time: 30 minutes.

. . . .

Per serving: Calories: 386   Fat: 14.2g   Saturated Fat: 3.6g   Protein: 42.1g
Carbohydrates: 21.5g   Fiber: 4.3g

Flounder Tostadas with Chunky Guacamole

Tostada shells are usually fried but in this clean eating version they're baked. Fish adds a healthy protein alternative to beef and cheese. The result is a spicy and smooth delicious meal.

Time-Saving Tip: Instead of making homemade guacamole, buy prepared guacamole from the deli section of your grocery store.

4 (100%) whole-wheat tortillas

3 tablespoons avocado oil

4 flounder fillets

1 teaspoon chili powder

½ teaspoon garlic powder

½ teaspoon salt

½ teaspoon black pepper

1 cup Chunky Guacamole (page 300)

2 cups shredded lettuce

1 cup chopped tomatoes

¼ cup chopped fresh cilantro

Lime wedges

1. Preheat the oven to 450°F.
2. Brush the tortillas with 2 tablespoons oil. Place them on a rimmed baking sheet. Bake for 10 minutes or until crisp, turning once.
3. Meanwhile, sprinkle the fish with chili powder, garlic powder, salt, and pepper. Heat the remaining 1 tablespoon of oil in a large nonstick skillet over medium-high heat. Add the fish, and cook for 4 to 5 minutes on each side or until the fish flakes easily when tested with a fork.
4. Spread ¼ cup of guacamole onto each tortilla. Top each with ½ cup of lettuce.
5. Flake the fish into chunks and divide it evenly among the tortillas. Top with the tomatoes and cilantro.
6. Serve with the lime wedges.

Serves 4. Prep time: 10 minutes. Cook time: 10 minutes. Total time: 20 minutes.

. . . .

Per serving: Calories: 221   Fat: 7.3g   Saturated Fat: 1.4g   Protein: 23.9g
Carbohydrates: 18.2g   Fiber: 4.6g

Blackened Catfish with Confetti Coleslaw

Gluten-Free
Dairy-Free

Tender catfish and zesty coleslaw are perfect companions. By making your own blackened seasoning, you know exactly what you're putting on your fish. Many commercial blackened seasonings include MSG in their ingredients mix. This seasoning keeps for up to 1 month in the pantry, so make extra if you'd like to season other seafood, poultry, or meat.

Make-Ahead Tip: Coleslaw is a great make-ahead recipe. The longer you let it refrigerate, the more the cabbage absorbs the dressing, making the salad tender and flavorful. Use a slotted spoon to serve it, because soaking it makes it a bit drippy.

For the catfish:
Coconut oil, for greasing
1 teaspoon smoked paprika
1 teaspoon dried thyme
¼ teaspoon garlic powder
½ teaspoon freshly ground
    black pepper
½ teaspoon salt
¼ teaspoon cayenne pepper
¼ teaspoon dried oregano
4 catfish fillets

For the coleslaw:
¼ cup Homemade Mayonnaise
    (page 288)
1 tablespoon white wine vinegar
1 tablespoon honey
½ teaspoon Dijon mustard
½ teaspoon salt
½ teaspoon freshly ground
    black pepper
4 cups shredded coleslaw mix
1 red bell pepper, thinly sliced
¼ cup chopped fresh parsley
Lemon wedges

To make the catfish:
1. Preheat the broiler.
2. Coat a rimmed baking sheet with coconut oil.
3. In a small bowl, combine the paprika, thyme, garlic powder, black pepper, salt, cayenne pepper, and oregano. Rub the mixture evenly on the fillets.

continued ▶

4. Place the fillets on the baking pan. Broil the fish 5 inches from heat for 6 to 8 minutes, or until the fish flakes easily when tested with a fork.

To make the coleslaw:

1. In a large bowl, whisk together the mayonnaise, vinegar, honey, mustard, salt, and pepper.
2. Add the coleslaw mix, bell pepper, and parsley. Toss well to coat. Cover and chill until ready to serve.
3. Serve the catfish and coleslaw with lemon wedges.

Serves 4. Prep time: 15 minutes. Cooking time: 10 minutes. Total time: 25 minutes.

. . . .

Per serving: Calories: 262   Fat: 12.7g   Saturated Fat: 2g   Protein: 11.4g
Carbohydrates: 25.9g   Fiber: 3.1g

Honey-Tamari Salmon with Rice and Snow Peas

Gluten-Free
Dairy-Free

Honey and tamari give the salmon a delicious sweet-salty teriyaki flavor. You can marinate the salmon up to 2 hours, if you'd like. It only improves the flavor. Steamed rice and steamed snow peas round out this Asian meal.

3 tablespoons tamari or coconut aminos

2 tablespoons honey

1½ tablespoons brown rice vinegar

1 garlic clove, minced

1 teaspoon grated fresh ginger

1½ pounds center-cut salmon fillets

1 cup uncooked brown rice

1½ pounds snow peas, trimmed

1. In a medium bowl, whisk together the tamari, honey, vinegar, garlic, and ginger. Place the salmon in a large zip-top plastic freezer bag. Pour 3 tablespoons of the marinade over the salmon. Marinate the salmon in the refrigerator for 15 minutes.
2. Prepare the rice according to the package directions, then keep the rice warm.
3. Preheat the broiler.
4. Line a rimmed baking sheet with aluminum foil. Place the salmon on the pan. Broil 5 inches from the heat for 8 to 10 minutes or until done.
5. Meanwhile, place the snow peas in a steamer basket in a saucepan over simmering water. Cover and steam for 3 minutes or until crisp-tender.
6. Place the salmon and rice on serving plates and drizzle with the reserved marinade. Serve with the snow peas.

Serves 4. Prep time: 10 minutes. Cooking time: 40 minutes.
Total time: 50 minutes (plus 15 minutes to marinate).

. . . .

Per serving: Calories: 576   Fat: 15.7g   Saturated Fat: 2.6g   Protein: 46.2g
Carbohydrates: 59.1g   Fiber: 5.6g

Steamed Mussels in Tomato-Fennel Broth

Mussels are delicious and are easier to prepare than you may think. This classic recipe will convince you to cook them often, as a starter or an entree. Before cooking them, scrub them well and remove the "beards" at the bottom of the shells. Discard any mussels with broken shells and any that won't close after they've been tapped.

Perfect Pairing: Serve these brothy mussels with baby arugula drizzled with Mustard-Thyme Vinaigrette (page 303).

2 tablespoons avocado oil

3 garlic cloves, minced

1 fennel bulb, thinly sliced, plus 2 tablespoons of the fennel fronds, chopped

½ cup fish stock

1 (28-ounce) can whole tomatoes, chopped

2 tablespoons chopped fresh parsley

½ cup water

2 pounds mussels, scrubbed

8 ounces 100% whole-grain French bread

1. In a large Dutch oven over medium heat, add the oil. Add the garlic and fennel bulb slices. Cook for 8 minutes or until the fennel is tender.
2. Add the fennel fronds and fish stock. Cook 2 minutes or until reduced by half. Add the tomatoes. Reduce the heat to low. Cover and simmer for 15 minutes.
3. Add the parsley, water, and mussels. Increase the temperature to medium-high. Cover and cook for 5 minutes or until the mussels open. Discard any unopened mussels.
4. Put the mussels in a large shallow bowl with the cooking liquid. Serve with thick slices of the French bread for dipping in the cooking liquid.

Serves 4. Prep time: 10 minutes. Cooking time: 30 minutes. Total time: 40 minutes.

Per serving: Calories: 417 Fat: 8.8g Saturated Fat: 1.3g Protein: 35.4g
Carbohydrates: 51.6g Fiber: 6.6g

Flounder Piccata with Sun-Dried Tomato Rice Pilaf

Piccata sauce is delicious with chicken and pork as well as with this fish. The tanginess of the lemon and saltiness of the capers give it a burst of flavor. Paired with sun-dried tomato pilaf, it's a wonderful meal for a weeknight or any night.

Ingredient Tip: Look for tender sun-dried tomatoes in the produce department of the store. You may use oil-packed or water-packed sun-dried tomatoes, or those in pouches that have the same consistency as dried apricots.

For the fish:

2 tablespoons coconut oil

4 flounder fillets

½ teaspoon salt

½ teaspoon freshly ground black pepper

2 tablespoons 100% whole-wheat pastry flour

¼ cup lemon juice

2 garlic cloves, minced

2 tablespoons drained capers

1 cup reduced-sodium chicken broth

For the rice:

2 tablespoons coconut oil

1 onion, chopped

1 cup short-grain brown rice

2 cups reduced-sodium chicken broth

¼ teaspoon salt

¼ teaspoon freshly ground black pepper

¼ cup chopped sun-dried tomatoes

2 tablespoons toasted pine nuts

2 tablespoons chopped fresh basil

To make the fish:

1. In a large nonstick skillet, heat the coconut oil. Sprinkle the fish evenly with salt and pepper, and dredge in the flour to lightly coat.
2. Cook the fish for 2 minutes on each side or until the fish flakes easily with a fork. Remove the fish from the skillet and keep warm.
3. Add the lemon juice, garlic, capers, and broth to the skillet. Cook for 2 minutes or until the liquid is reduced slightly.

To make the rice:

1. In a medium saucepan, heat the oil over medium heat. Add the onion and cook for 5 minutes or until tender.
2. Add the rice and cook for 2 minutes or until toasted.
3. Add the broth, salt, and pepper. Bring to a boil. Cover, reduce the heat to low, and simmer for 45 minutes or until the rice is done. Remove the rice from the heat and stir in the tomatoes and pine nuts. Fluff with a fork before serving.
4. Serve the fish alongside the rice, spooning sauce over both. Sprinkle with the basil.

Serves 4. Prep time: 10 minutes. Cooking time: 55 minutes. Total time: 1 hour, 5 minutes.

. . . .

Per serving: Calories: 838 Fat: 23.6g Saturated Fat: 14.4g Protein: 96.4g
Carbohydrates: 61.5g Fiber: 4.7g

Seared Scallops with Chimichurri and Roasted Smoked Paprika Potatoes

Sweet, tender, seared scallops are such a treat. Chimichurri sauce is a green herb sauce from Argentina that was originally used for meat but it is delicious with scallops. It's also perfect with steak, chicken, and fish.

Ingredient Tip: Be sure to buy dry-packed or chemical-free sea scallops instead of wet-packed ones. They will brown up nicely instead of releasing liquid as they cook, and they taste sweeter.

For the scallops:

½ cup fresh parsley

½ cup extra-virgin olive oil

2 tablespoons chopped
    fresh cilantro

2 tablespoons lemon juice

1 garlic clove

¼ teaspoon red pepper flakes

¼ teaspoon ground cumin

¼ teaspoon salt

2 tablespoons coconut oil

1½ pounds sea scallops

For the potatoes:

1½ pounds new potatoes,
    cut into wedges

2 tablespoons coconut oil,
    plus additional for greasing

1 teaspoon smoked paprika

½ teaspoon salt

½ teaspoon freshly ground
    black pepper

To make the scallops:

1. In a food processor, combine the parsley, olive oil, cilantro, lemon juice, garlic, red pepper flakes, cumin, and salt. Pulse until smooth.
2. Heat the oil in a large nonstick skillet over medium-high heat. Add the scallops. Cook for 2 to 3 minutes on each side or until done.

To make the potatoes:

1. Preheat the oven to 425°F.
2. Coat a rimmed baking sheet with coconut oil.
3. Combine the potatoes, 2 tablespoons of coconut oil, paprika, salt, and pepper on the prepared baking sheet; toss well to coat.
4. Bake for 20 to 25 minutes or until the potatoes are browned and tender.
5. Serve the scallops with the potatoes, spooning the chimichurri sauce over the scallops.

Serves 4. Prep time: 10 minutes. Cooking time: 20 minutes. Total time: 30 minutes.

. . . .

Per serving: Calories: 609   Fat: 40.5g   Saturated Fat: 15.6g   Protein: 31.9g
Carbohydrates: 32.2g   Fiber: 4.7g

Thai Shrimp and Snow Pea Curry

Gluten-Free
Dairy-Free

Red curry paste is a tasty ingredient that packs a punch of flavor in many dishes. You can find it in the Asian foods section at the market. Depending on how much heat you want, you may want to increase the amount of red curry paste used in the recipe.

Cooking Tip: Thaw the snow peas in a colander and drain. Pat them dry before adding them to the curry so they don't add extra moisture.

1 cup brown rice	1 tablespoon red curry paste
2 tablespoons coconut oil	¾ cup coconut milk
2 garlic cloves, minced	¼ cup lime juice
2 tablespoons grated peeled fresh ginger	1 tablespoon fish sauce
1½ pounds peeled and deveined large shrimp	1 (10-ounce) package frozen snow peas, thawed
	¼ cup chopped fresh cilantro

1. Cook the rice according to the package directions, then fluff with a fork.
2. In a large nonstick skillet over medium heat, heat the oil. Add the garlic and ginger and cook for 1 minute or until tender. Add the shrimp. Cook for 2 minutes or until the shrimp turn pink but are not cooked all the way through.
3. In a small bowl, whisk together the curry paste, coconut milk, lime juice, and fish sauce. Add the curry mixture to the skillet along with the snow peas, and stir to combine. Cook for 5 minutes or until bubbly.
4. Serve the curry hot over the cooked rice, and sprinkle with cilantro.

Serves 4. Prep time: 10 minutes. Cooking time: 40 minutes. Total time: 50 minutes.

....

Per serving: Calories: 510   Fat: 20.8g   Saturated Fat: 15.9g   Protein: 34g
Carbohydrates: 48.2g   Fiber: 3.8g

Grilled Scallops with Mango Salsa and Grilled Zucchini

Tropical mango salsa pairs well with sweet grilled scallops. It also makes a beautiful and colorful dish when you add the zucchini. The salsa can be made ahead for this dish, or served with Baked Tortilla Chips (page 133) as an appetizer or snack. Store the salsa in the refrigerator in an airtight container for up to 3 days. You might want to serve this dish with steamed brown rice.

Cooking Tip: Mangos can sometimes be difficult to peel and chop. Before peeling, try removing the egg-shaped pit with a sharp knife. Start at the stem end and follow the curved shape of the seed. Score the flesh with a knife and carefully slice it away from the pit.

For the salsa:
1 mango, peeled and
    finely chopped
1 avocado, finely chopped
1 jalapeño pepper, seeded
    and minced
⅓ cup finely chopped
    red onion
1 tablespoon lime juice
⅓ cup chopped fresh cilantro
¼ teaspoon salt
¼ teaspoon freshly ground
    black pepper
For the scallops:
1½ pounds sea scallops, rinsed
    and patted dry

2 tablespoons coconut oil
½ teaspoon salt
½ teaspoon freshly ground
    black pepper
For the zucchini:
2 medium zucchini,
    cut lengthwise into
    ¼-inch-thick strips
1 tablespoon coconut oil
½ teaspoon salt
½ teaspoon freshly ground
    black pepper

To make the salsa:

In a medium bowl, stir together the mango, avocado, jalapeño, red onion, lime juice, cilantro, salt, and pepper. Set aside.

To make the scallops:

1. Preheat the grill to medium-high heat.
2. Brush the scallops evenly with the oil. Sprinkle them with the salt and pepper.
3. Grill the scallops for 2 to 3 minutes on each side or until just cooked through. Do not overcook.

To make the zucchini:

1. Brush the zucchini with oil; sprinkle with salt and pepper.
2. Grill the zucchini alongside the scallops for 3 to 4 minutes or until tender.
3. To serve, plate the scallops and zucchini and spoon a dollop of salsa on the scallops. Pass the extra salsa.

Serves 4. Prep time: 15 minutes. Cooking time: 10 minutes. Total time: 25 minutes.

....

Per serving: Calories: 385   Fat: 21.6g   Saturated Fat: 11.1g   Protein: 31.2g
Carbohydrates: 19.2g   Fiber: 5.9g

Halibut with Warm Tomato Topping and Green Beans with Shallot Vinaigrette

Halibut is a large flat fish with a low fat content. When cooked, it has a delicious firm, flaky texture. This recipe has a simple sauce to bring out the clean taste of the fish. Be sure to buy Pacific halibut because Atlantic halibut are overfished.

Time-Saving Tip: This dinner comes together in less than 30 minutes when you do some smart planning in the kitchen. Steam the green beans while you are cooking the halibut to have dinner on the table in no time.

For the halibut:
4 (6-ounce) halibut fillets
½ teaspoon salt
½ teaspoon freshly ground
    black pepper
2 tablespoons avocado oil
2 cups grape tomatoes
2 tablespoons
    balsamic vinegar

For the green beans:
1 pound fresh green
    beans, trimmed
1 shallot, minced
1 tablespoon chopped
    fresh thyme
1 tablespoon extra-virgin
    olive oil
1 tablespoon white
    wine vinegar
1 teaspoon grainy
    Dijon mustard
¼ teaspoon salt
¼ teaspoon freshly ground
    black pepper

To make the halibut:

1. Sprinkle the halibut with salt and pepper.
2. In a large nonstick skillet over medium-high heat, heat the avocado oil. Cook the halibut for 4 to 5 minutes on each side or until the fish flakes easily when tested with a fork. Remove the fish from the pan to a large serving dish and keep warm.

3. Add the tomatoes to the pan. Cook for 4 minutes or until the tomatoes begin to burst. Add the balsamic vinegar, stir, and cook for 1 more minute or until the tomatoes are tender and form a sauce.
4. Spoon the tomato sauce over the fish.

To make the green beans:
1. Place the green beans in a steamer basket in a medium saucepan filled with simmering water over medium-high heat. Cover and cook for 5 minutes or until the beans are crisp-tender. Transfer them to a serving platter.
2. Meanwhile, in a small bowl, whisk together the shallot, thyme, oil, vinegar, mustard, salt, and pepper. Spoon the vinaigrette over the green beans.
3. Place the halibut and green beans on warm plates and serve hot.

Serves 4. Prep time: 10 minutes. Cooking time: 15 minutes. Total time: 25 minutes.

. . . .

Per serving: Calories: 334   Fat: 9.7g   Saturated Fat: 1.5g   Protein: 48.4g
Carbohydrates: 12.6g   Fiber: 5.4g

10

Meat and Poultry Dinners

Lemon-Garlic Roasted Chicken with Steamed Broccoli and Wild Rice

This lemon-garlic roasted chicken is supreme. The skin on the chicken holds in the moisture and flavorful seasonings, and it crisps up nicely from browning the chicken before it bakes. If you'd like to pare a few grams of fat off this recipe, feel free to remove the skin after the chicken is baked. Or not. We won't tell.

Ingredient Tip: Herbes de Provence is a unique spice blend hailing from France that includes a mixture of savory, marjoram, rosemary, thyme, oregano, and lavender. You can buy this blend in the spice aisle of the grocery store. Or, substitute Italian seasoning if you'd prefer.

For the chicken:
1 whole chicken (about
    4 pounds)
1 teaspoon salt
1 teaspoon freshly ground
    black pepper
2 teaspoons herbes de
    Provence
2 teaspoons lemon zest
¼ cup lemon juice
2 garlic heads, tops cut off to
    reveal cloves
1 lemon, halved
2 tablespoons butter, cut into
    several pieces

4 sprigs fresh rosemary
    (optional)
For the broccoli:
2 pounds broccoli, cut into
    florets and bite-size pieces
2 tablespoons extra-virgin
    olive oil
½ teaspoon salt
½ teaspoon freshly ground
    black pepper
For the wild rice:
1 cup uncooked wild rice

To make the chicken:

1. Preheat the oven to 425°F.
2. Loosen the skin from the chicken. In a small bowl, combine the salt, pepper, herbes de Provence, and lemon zest. Rub the mixture underneath the skin of the chicken.
3. Place the chicken breast-side up on a roasting pan and sprinkle the lemon juice all over the top; arrange the garlic and lemon halves around the chicken in the pan.
4. Roast the chicken for about 90 minutes, until the juices run clear when pierced between the leg and thigh with a knife. Remove the chicken from the pan, top it with the butter and rosemary sprigs (if using), tent with foil, and let rest for 15 minutes.

To make the broccoli:

1. Place the broccoli in a steamer basket in a saucepan over simmering water. Cover and steam for 5 minutes or until crisp-tender.
2. Transfer the broccoli to serving bowl; stir in the olive oil, salt, and pepper until well coated.

To make the wild rice:

1. Cook the rice according to the package directions. Fluff it with a fork.
2. Carve the chicken as desired and serve it with the broccoli and rice.

Serves 8. Prep time: 15 minutes. Cooking time: 1 hour, 30 minutes.
Total time: 1 hour, 45 minutes (plus 15 minutes to rest).

. . . .

Per serving: Calories: 521   Fat: 14.5g   Saturated Fat: 4.5g   Protein: 72.7g
Carbohydrates: 23.3g   Fiber: 4.5g

Skillet-Barbecued Chicken with Mustard Green Bean–Potato Salad

This yummy skillet-barbecued chicken is easy to make, and is especially tasty with green bean–potato salad alongside. The recipe can easily be reduced to four servings. Cook the six chicken breasts as directed and then save two to be used in other recipes during the week.

Time-Saving Tip: This recipe uses three homemade condiments that can be found in the Kitchen Staples chapter (page 287). These condiments can be made ahead and stored in the refrigerator to reduce prep time for cooking this meal.

For the chicken:

6 boneless skinless
   chicken breasts
½ teaspoon salt
½ teaspoon freshly ground
   black pepper
2 tablespoons coconut oil
1 onion, halved and sliced
1 cup Smoky-Sweet Barbecue
   Sauce (page 291)

For the potato salad:

1½ pounds new potatoes, cut
   into 1-inch chunks
2 cups frozen green beans
½ cup Mustard-Thyme
   Vinaigrette (page 303)
¼ cup chopped fresh basil
2 tablespoons Homemade
   Mayonnaise (page 288)

To make the chicken:

1. Sprinkle the chicken with salt and pepper. In a large nonstick skillet over medium heat, heat the coconut oil.
2. Cook the chicken for 5 to 6 minutes on each side or until cooked through. Remove to a serving platter and keep warm.
3. Add the onion to the skillet. Cook for 5 minutes or until tender. Stir in the barbecue sauce. Cook for 2 more minutes or until bubbly. Spoon the sauce over the chicken.

To make the potato salad:

1. Place the potatoes in a pot of salted water over high heat. Bring to a boil. Cook for 10 to 15 minutes or until tender. Add the green beans during the last 3 minutes of cooking.
2. Drain the potatoes and green beans and run under cold water to cool. Transfer the mixture to a large serving bowl.
3. In a small bowl, whisk together the vinaigrette, basil, and mayonnaise. Pour the dressing over the potato–green bean mixture, and toss well to coat.
4. Serve the chicken hot, with the potato salad alongside.

Serves 6. Prep time: 20 minutes. Cooking time: 20 minutes. Total time: 40 minutes.

....

Per serving: Calories: 845   Fat: 29.9g   Saturated Fat: 9.7g   Protein: 57.1g
Carbohydrates: 86.9g   Fiber: 12g

Chicken Breasts Stuffed with Roasted Red Peppers, Olives, and Feta

This Mediterranean-inspired chicken dish is so tasty. The stuffing mixture, combining the crunch of bell pepper with salty and tangy feta and olives, is a guaranteed palate pleaser, ideal for use in other recipes, too, like with boneless pork chops or turkey breasts. You can also stir it into farro, quinoa, or brown rice for a quick make-and-take lunch.

Perfect Pairing: Serve this dish with steamed broccoli or steamed green beans to round out the meal.

4 boneless skinless
   chicken breasts
½ cup chopped roasted
   red peppers
½ cup crumbled feta cheese
½ cup chopped
   Kalamata olives
2 tablespoons chopped
   fresh basil

1 teaspoon salt
1 teaspoon freshly ground
   black pepper
2 tablespoons avocado oil
2 cups 100% whole-wheat
   orzo pasta
2 tablespoons lemon juice

1. Preheat the oven to 350°F.
2. Cut a horizontal slit into each chicken breast without cutting it completely in half. In a medium bowl, combine the red peppers, feta, olives, and basil. Stuff the mixture into each slit. Use toothpicks to close.
3. Sprinkle the chicken with ½ teaspoon of salt and pepper. Heat the oil in a large oven-proof skillet over medium-high heat. Brown the chicken for 2 to 3 minutes on each side.
4. Transfer the skillet to the oven. Bake the chicken for 10 to 15 minutes or until done. Transfer the chicken to a warm serving platter.

5. While the chicken cooks, prepare the orzo according to the package directions. Drain, and transfer the orzo to a serving bowl. Stir in the lemon juice and remaining ½ teaspoon each of salt and pepper.
6. Serve the stuffed hot chicken breasts with the orzo alongside.

Serves 4. Prep time: 10 minutes. Cooking time: 20 minutes. Total time: 30 minutes.

. . . .

Per serving: Calories: 601   Fat: 20.3g   Saturated Fat: 6.7g   Protein: 58.4g
Carbohydrates: 45.3g   Fiber: 3.4g

Chicken Pasta Puttanesca

This zesty Italian favorite can be made with most ingredients you already have on hand. The olives and capers give a briny flavor to the sweet tomatoes, and the spicy kick from the crushed red pepper can be tamed or pumped up depending on how you like it. Garnish the pasta with fresh parsley, if desired.

Perfect Pair: This dish goes well with a classic Caesar salad. To make, chop romaine lettuce and drizzle it with Creamy Caesar Dressing (page 304). For a modern twist, grill halved romaine hearts before drizzling them with the dressing.

12 ounces 100% whole-grain penne

4 boneless skinless chicken breasts, cut into 1-inch pieces

½ teaspoon salt

½ teaspoon freshly ground black pepper

2 tablespoons avocado oil

2 garlic cloves, minced

¼ teaspoon crushed red pepper

1 (28-ounce) can crushed tomatoes in puree

½ cup chopped pitted Kalamata olives

2 tablespoons capers

1. Cook the pasta according to the package directions; drain, and keep warm.
2. Sprinkle the chicken evenly with salt and pepper. Heat the oil in a Dutch oven over medium heat. Brown the chicken for 5 minutes, stirring occasionally.
3. Add the garlic and crushed red pepper. Cook for 2 minutes or until the garlic is tender.
4. Add the tomatoes, olives, and capers. Bring to a simmer. Cook for 5 minutes or until the sauce is bubbly.
5. Add the cooked pasta to the sauce; toss well to coat. Divide the chicken pasta among serving plates.

Serves 4. Prep time: 10 minutes. Cooking time: 15 minutes. Total time: 25 minutes.

. . . .

Per serving: Calories: 710   Fat: 17.6g   Saturated Fat: 3.9g   Protein: 63.6g
Carbohydrates: 76.1g   Fiber: 11.9g

Grilled Honey-Mustard Chicken with Marinated Tomatoes and Cucumbers

The chicken breasts in this recipe are marinated in the simplest way possible: placed in a zip-lock bag with oil and vinegar, mustard, and honey. The result is a deliciously clean and simple chicken that is versatile enough to be used in other dishes.

Time-Saving Tip: Use the extra three cooked chicken breasts for other recipes during the week. Whether for lunch with the Chicken-Pesto BLT (page 129) or Chicken-Quinoa Salad with Oranges, Olives, and Feta (page 118), or for help getting dinner on the table quickly, these chicken breasts serve double-duty.

For the chicken:

¼ cup honey

¼ cup grainy Dijon mustard

2 tablespoons white wine vinegar

2 tablespoons avocado oil, plus additional for greasing

7 boneless skinless chicken breasts

¾ teaspoon salt

½ teaspoon freshly ground black pepper

For the marinated tomatoes and cucumbers:

3 tomatoes, cut into wedges

2 cucumbers, peeled and cut into half-moons

1 red onion, halved and sliced

⅓ cup balsamic vinegar

3 tablespoons extra-virgin olive oil

2 tablespoons honey

½ teaspoon salt

½ teaspoon freshly ground black pepper

3 tablespoons chopped fresh basil

To make the chicken:

1. Whisk together the honey, Dijon mustard, vinegar, and oil. Place the chicken in a large zip-top freezer bag; pour the marinade over the chicken. Seal and refrigerate for at least 30 minutes or up to 2 hours.
2. Preheat the grill to medium-high heat.
3. Remove the chicken from the marinade and discard the marinade. Sprinkle the chicken with salt and pepper.
4. Place the chicken on a well-oiled grill rack and grill for 4 to 5 minutes on each side.

To make the marinated tomatoes and cucumbers:

1. In a large bowl, combine the tomatoes, cucumbers, and red onion. Whisk together the vinegar, oil, honey, salt, pepper, and basil; pour the dressing over the tomato mixture, tossing well to coat.
2. Cover and refrigerate for at least 30 minutes or up to 2 hours before serving.
3. Serve the chicken with the marinated vegetables alongside.

Serves 7. Prep time: 15 minutes. Cooking time: 10 minutes.
Total time: 25 minutes (plus 30 minutes to marinate).

Per serving: Calories: 486   Fat: 21.1g   Saturated Fat: 5.3g   Protein: 51.2g
Carbohydrates: 22.2g   Fiber: 1.8g

Panko-Pecan Crusted Chicken Tenders with Steamed Broccoli

You'll feel great about serving this delicious, kid-friendly (and adult-friendly) version of chicken fingers to your family. Instead of deep-frying, these oven-baked tenders get their crunch from 100% whole-wheat panko and crispy chopped pecans. Served with clean eating approved honey-mustard sauce, this recipe is sure to be requested by your family over and over again.

Time-Saving Tip: Every now and then, supermarkets put chicken tenders on sale. When they do, grab a few packages to put in the freezer to help you save an extra five minutes of prep time with this recipe.

For the chicken tenders:

Coconut oil for greasing

1½ pounds boneless skinless chicken breasts, cut into strips

1 teaspoon Italian seasoning

1 teaspoon garlic powder

½ teaspoon salt

½ teaspoon freshly ground black pepper

1 cup 100% whole wheat panko bread crumbs

½ cup finely chopped pecans

2 eggs, lightly beaten

½ cup 100% whole-wheat pastry flour

For the broccoli:

1 (16-ounce) package frozen broccoli florets

2 tablespoons extra-virgin olive oil

½ teaspoon salt

½ teaspoon freshly ground black pepper

½ cup Honey-Mustard Dipping Sauce (page 289)

To make the chicken tenders:

1. Preheat the oven to 350°F.
2. Coat a rimmed baking sheet with the coconut oil; place it in the oven while it preheats.

3. Season the chicken with Italian seasoning, garlic powder, salt, and pepper.
4. Combine the panko and pecans in a shallow dish. Place the eggs in another shallow dish; place the flour in a third shallow dish.
5. Dredge the chicken in the flour; shake off the excess. Dip the chicken in the egg and then coat it in the panko mixture. Place the chicken tenders on the preheated baking sheet.
6. Bake the chicken for 12 to 15 minutes or until golden brown, turning once halfway through baking.

To make the broccoli:
1. Place the broccoli in a steamer basket in a medium saucepan over simmering water. Cover and steam for 5 minutes or until crisp-tender.
2. Transfer the broccoli to a serving bowl; add the olive oil, salt, and pepper, tossing well to coat.
3. Serve the chicken with the honey-mustard sauce and with broccoli on the side.

Serves 4. Prep time: 20 minutes. Cooking time: 15 minutes. Total time: 35 minutes.

. . . .

Per serving: Calories: 640 Fat: 22.8g Saturated Fat: 5.2g Protein: 59.6g
Carbohydrates: 43.8g Fiber: 6.1g

Tandoori Chicken Kabobs

Hailing from India, tandoori chicken is a great go-to meal that's quick and easy to prepare. This recipe calls for a homemade tandoori seasoning, but you can also buy tandoori seasoning from online specialty gourmet stores, like Penzeys Spices.

Perfect Pairing: Serve these kabobs with grilled zucchini and steamed brown basmati rice to round out the meal.

1½ cups plain Greek yogurt

2 tablespoons lemon juice

2 teaspoons smoked paprika

½ teaspoon ground cumin

½ teaspoon ground coriander

½ teaspoon salt

½ teaspoon freshly ground
    black pepper

¼ teaspoon ground ginger

¼ teaspoon cayenne pepper

3 garlic cloves, minced

1½ pounds boneless skinless
    chicken breasts, cut into
    2-inch cubes

1. In a medium bowl, whisk together the yogurt, lemon juice, paprika, cumin, coriander, salt, black pepper, ginger, cayenne pepper, and garlic.
2. Place the chicken in a large zip-top plastic freezer bag; add the yogurt mixture, turning to coat evenly.
3. Cover and refrigerate for 4 to 8 hours. Remove the chicken from the marinade, discarding marinade.
4. Preheat the grill to medium-high heat.
5. Thread the chicken onto 8 (12-inch) skewers.
6. Grill the chicken for 6 to 8 minutes, turning occasionally, or until done.
7. Serve the kabobs on the skewers.

Serves 4. Prep time: 20 minutes. Cooking time: 10 minutes.
Total time: 30 minutes (plus marinating time).

. . . .

Per serving: Calories: 413   Fat: 16.7g   Saturated Fat: 5.8g   Protein: 56.8g
Carbohydrates: 5.7g   Fiber: 0.6g

Pork and Bok Choy Stir-Fry

Gluten-Free
Dairy-Free

There's no need to get Chinese take-out when you can make this satisfying dish at home. For a different twist, try chicken, beef, or even tofu in place of the pork.

Ingredient Tip: Tender baby bok choy is a great addition to this dish and adds vitamins A and C. Be sure to wash each stalk thoroughly because sand tends to sneak between the leaf layers.

1 cup uncooked brown rice

1 tablespoon arrowroot powder

1 tablespoon honey

¼ cup orange juice

¼ cup tamari

1 tablespoon brown rice vinegar

1 tablespoon dark sesame oil

1 tablespoon grated fresh ginger

2 garlic cloves, minced

2 tablespoons coconut oil

1 pound pork tenderloin, cut into thin strips

3 baby bok choy, cut into 1-inch pieces

1 red bell pepper, sliced

1. Cook the rice according to the package directions; keep warm.
2. In a small saucepan, whisk together the arrowroot powder, honey, orange juice, tamari, vinegar, sesame oil, ginger, and garlic. Cook over medium heat, stirring constantly, for 2 minutes or until the mixture thickens. Set aside.
3. In a large nonstick skillet over medium-high heat, heat 1 tablespoon of oil. Add the pork to the skillet. Cook for 5 to 6 minutes or until the pork is browned. Remove the pork from skillet and keep warm.
4. Heat the remaining 1 tablespoon of oil in the skillet. Add the bok choy and bell pepper. Cook for 3 minutes or until crisp-tender.
5. Return the pork to the skillet. Add the reserved sauce, tossing to coat. Stir-fry completely.
6. Serve the pork and vegetables over the cooked rice.

Serves 4. Prep time: 15 minutes. Cooking time: 40 minutes. Total time: 55 minutes.

....

Per serving: Calories: 577   Fat: 16g   Saturated Fat: 8g   Protein: 45.3g
Carbohydrates: 66.7g   Fiber: 9g

Pulled Pork Sliders with Vinegar Slaw

Take a trip to the South with this classic pulled pork and coleslaw combo. This recipe uses leftovers from dishes like Braised Pork Loin with Dried Figs and Roasted Asparagus (page 238). If you don't have leftover pork, you may substitute shredded chicken. Or, stop by your favorite barbecue joint and pick up a pound of pulled pork without their (sugary) sauce.

Ingredient Variation: If you prefer creamy coleslaw, substitute the Confetti Coleslaw (page 201) for this vinegar variety. You may also serve the slaw on the side, if you prefer.

3 tablespoons avocado oil

2 tablespoons apple
   cider vinegar

1 tablespoon honey

½ teaspoon salt

½ teaspoon freshly ground
   black pepper

¼ teaspoon dry mustard

¼ teaspoon ground cumin

3 cups shredded coleslaw mix

3 cups shredded cooked pork

½ cup Smoky-Sweet Barbecue
   Sauce (page 291)

12 whole-wheat slider buns

1. In a large bowl, whisk together the oil, vinegar, honey, salt, pepper, mustard, and cumin. Add the coleslaw mix and toss well to coat. Cover and refrigerate for 1 hour.

2. In a large skillet over medium heat, warm the pulled pork with the barbecue sauce for 10 minutes.

3. Spoon the pork onto the buns and top each with coleslaw. Serve.

Serves 4. Prep time: 10 minutes. Cooking time: 10 minutes.
Total time: 20 minutes (plus 1 hour to chill).

....

Per serving: Calories: 409   Fat: 9.5g   Saturated Fat: 2.3g   Protein: 34.2g
Carbohydrates: 46.2g   Fiber: 4.8g

Moroccan Braised Chicken Thighs and Minted Couscous with Peas

Moroccan flavors of turmeric and cumin are slow cooked into the juicy chicken thighs for a fall-off-the-bone result that's delicious served over mint- and pea-studded couscous. Making this dish in a slow cooker is an easy, effective way to cook it. Slow cookers are often associated with cold weather months, but they are great for hot weather cooking, too! They prevent the need to heat up the oven so you keep your kitchen cool.

Cooking Tip: If you don't want to use a slow cooker for this recipe, you can easily use a Dutch oven instead. Add the seasoned broth mixture to the Dutch oven after you've browned the chicken. Cook the chicken thighs on the stove top over medium-low heat for 1 hour or until the thighs and dates are tender and done.

For the chicken thighs:

2 pounds skinless bone-in chicken thighs

½ teaspoon salt

½ teaspoon freshly ground black pepper

2 tablespoons coconut oil

2 garlic cloves, minced

1 tablespoon grated fresh ginger

1 teaspoon ground cumin

1 teaspoon ground turmeric

1½ cups chopped pitted dates

1 (14.5-ounce) can reduced-sodium chicken broth

For the couscous:

2 cups uncooked 100% whole-wheat couscous

2 cups frozen green peas

2 tablespoons chopped fresh mint

1 tablespoon freshly squeezed lemon juice

1 teaspoon fresh lemon zest

½ teaspoon salt

½ teaspoon freshly ground black pepper

To make the chicken thighs:

1. Sprinkle the chicken evenly with the salt and pepper.
2. In a large nonstick skillet over medium-high heat, heat the oil. Brown the chicken for 2 to 3 minutes on each side.
3. Transfer the chicken to a 5- to 6-quart slow cooker. In a medium bowl, stir together the garlic, ginger, cumin, turmeric, dates, and chicken broth. Pour the mixture over the chicken in the slow cooker.
4. Cover and cook on the low setting for 5 hours, or until the chicken is done.

To make the couscous:

1. Prepare the couscous according to the package directions. During standing time, add the peas, mint, lemon juice, lemon zest, salt, and pepper.
2. Fluff with a fork before serving topped with the chicken thighs.

Serves 4. Prep time: 15 minutes. Cooking time: 5 hours, 10 minutes.
Total time: 5 hours, 25 minutes.

. . . .

Per serving: Calories: 925   Fat: 17.8g   Saturated Fat: 8.3g   Protein: 63.8g
Carbohydrates: 131.9g   Fiber: 14.5g

Turkey Cutlets with Fresh Cranberry Sauce and Mashed Sweet Potatoes

Enjoy this Thanksgiving-inspired comforting meal any time of year. During the fall and winter, you can find fresh cranberries in the produce department of the grocery store. For other times of the year, look for frozen cranberries where the other frozen fruit is located.

Perfect Pairing: Complete this colorful meal with steamed Brussels sprouts or Green Beans with Shallot Vinaigrette (page 214).

For the turkey:

2 cups fresh or frozen cranberries, thawed

1 tablespoon honey

¼ cup freshly squeezed orange juice (1 orange)

1 teaspoon orange zest

1 teaspoon grated fresh ginger

1 pound turkey cutlets

½ teaspoon salt

½ teaspoon freshly ground black pepper

2 tablespoons butter

For the mashed sweet potatoes:

1½ pounds sweet potatoes

2 tablespoons butter

1 tablespoon maple syrup

½ teaspoon salt

½ teaspoon freshly ground black pepper

To make the turkey:

1. In a medium saucepan, combine the cranberries, honey, orange juice, orange zest, and ginger. Bring to a boil. Reduce the heat and simmer for 10 minutes or until the cranberries begin to pop and the sauce thickens.

2. While the sauce cooks, sprinkle the turkey with salt and pepper.

3. In a large nonstick skillet over medium-high heat, melt the butter. Cook the turkey for 2 to 3 minutes on each side or until done.

To make the mashed sweet potatoes:

1. Preheat the oven to 425°F.
2. Place the sweet potatoes on a rimmed baking sheet. Bake for 30 to 35 minutes or until the sweet potatoes are very tender.
3. Let cool for 5 minutes. Peel the sweet potatoes and place them in a serving bowl. Add the butter, maple syrup, salt, and pepper. Mash the sweet potatoes with a potato masher to desired smoothness.
4. Serve the cranberry sauce over the turkey with the mashed sweet potatoes on the side.

Serves 4. Prep time: 10 minutes. Cooking time: 30 minutes. Total time: 40 minutes.

....

Per serving: Calories: 305   Fat: 11.6g   Saturated Fat: 5.5g   Protein: 34g
Carbohydrates: 16g   Fiber: 3.4g

Braised Pork Loin with Dried Figs and Roasted Asparagus

Dried fruit often works well with meat and poultry because it adds an unexpected sweetness and holds up well for long periods of cooking. In this spice-rubbed pork dish figs are the surprise ingredient. Prepare this recipe in a slow cooker for a very moist and succulent dinner.

Halve It: If you're not in the mood for leftovers, this dish can easily be halved. Be sure to reduce your slow cooker size to 3½ to 4 quarts and reduce the cooking time to around 5 hours.

1 (3¼-pound) boneless pork loin roast, trimmed and halved crosswise

2 teaspoons freshly ground black pepper

1½ teaspoons salt

1 teaspoon dry mustard

1 teaspoon dried thyme

3 tablespoons avocado oil

1 red onion, halved and thinly sliced

3 carrots, finely chopped

1 (14.5-ounce) can reduced-sodium chicken broth

1 cup dried figs

2 bay leaves

2 tablespoons arrowroot powder

1½ pounds asparagus, trimmed

1. Cut the roast in half crosswise. Rub 1½ teaspoons pepper, 1 teaspoon salt, dry mustard, and thyme over the pork.

2. In a large Dutch oven over medium-high heat, add 1 tablespoon of avocado oil to the pan and swirl to coat. Add the pork, browning on all sides, about 10 minutes. Place the pork in a 5-quart slow cooker. Add the onion and carrots to the Dutch oven; sauté for 5 minutes or until the vegetables are golden. Stir in the chicken broth, scraping the pan to loosen browned bits. Pour the mixture over the pork in the slow cooker; add the figs and bay leaves. Cover and cook on low for 6 hours or until the pork is tender.

3. Remove the pork from the slow cooker; reserve the cooking liquid in the slow cooker. Set the pork aside; keep warm. Increase the heat to high.
4. In a small bowl, combine the arrowroot and 2 tablespoons of water. Stir well, then add it to the cooking liquid. Cook uncovered, for 15 minutes or until the mixture is thick, stirring frequently. Discard the bay leaves.
5. While the pork cooks, heat the oven to 425°F. Arrange the asparagus in a single layer on a rimmed baking sheet brushed with 1 tablespoon of avocado oil; toss the asparagus with the remaining 1 tablespoon of avocado oil, remaining ½ teaspoon of salt, and remaining ½ teaspoon of pepper. Bake for 15 minutes or until the asparagus is browned and crisp-tender.
6. Slice the pork and serve it with the sauce and asparagus.

Serves 8. Prep time: 15 minutes. Cook time: 6 hours, 15 minutes.
Total time: 6 hours, 30 minutes.

. . . .

Per serving: Calories: 389   Fat: 7.7g   Saturated Fat: 2.5g   Protein: 52.6g
Carbohydrates: 27.2g   Fiber: 5.9g

Cajun Pork Chops with Grilled Okra and Creamed Corn

This Southern-inspired meal highlights the fresh flavors of summer in the best way. Smoky, spicy pork chops are the perfect accompaniment to grilled okra and fresh, sweet creamed corn. If you don't think you're an okra fan, this dish might just change your opinion. Grilling the okra cooks it to delicately browned perfection.

Cooking Tip: Skewer the okra with double skewers (a skewer at each end) to help it stay steady on the grill. If you're using wooden skewers, don't forget to soak them for at least 30 minutes in water first.

For the pork chops:
½ teaspoon dried thyme
½ teaspoon dried oregano
½ teaspoon smoked paprika
½ teaspoon salt
½ teaspoon freshly ground
    black pepper
½ teaspoon cayenne pepper
4 pork loin chops

For the okra:
1 pound fresh okra
2 tablespoons avocado oil

½ teaspoon salt
½ teaspoon freshly ground
    black pepper

For the creamed corn:
4 ears corn, shucked
    and cleaned
¾ cup reduced-sodium
    chicken broth
2 tablespoons butter
¼ teaspoon salt
¼ teaspoon freshly ground
    black pepper

To make the pork chops:
1. Preheat the grill to medium-high heat.
2. In a small bowl, combine the thyme, oregano, paprika, salt, black pepper, and cayenne pepper. Rub the mixture evenly on the pork chops.
3. Grill the pork chops for 4 to 5 minutes on each side or until done.

continued ▶

To make the okra:

1. In a large bowl, combine the okra, oil, salt, and pepper. Thread the okra on double skewers.
2. While the pork chops are grilling, grill the okra for 3 to 4 minutes on each side or until tender.

To make the creamed corn:

1. Cut the tips off the corn. Stand an ear in a wide shallow bowl and cut off the kernels; use the back of the knife to scrape the pulp from the corn cobs. Repeat with each ear.
2. In a medium saucepan, combine the corn, broth, butter, salt, and pepper; bring to a boil.
3. Reduce the heat and simmer for 10 to 12 minutes or until the corn is tender and thickened, stirring frequently.
4. Serve the pork chops, corn, and okra immediately.

Serves 4. Prep time: 20 minutes. Cooking time: 10 minutes. Total time: 30 minutes.

Per serving: Calories: 358   Fat: 17.7g   Saturated Fat: 7.6g   Protein: 28.3g
Carbohydrates: 24g   Fiber: 6.1g

Chicken and Broccoli Tetrazzini

This traditional favorite is usually loaded with fat, calories, and processed foods, but it's been revised for this clean eating version. Even better, it mostly uses ingredients you've already got on hand. Pick up a rotisserie natural chicken at the grocery store to make prep time super fast.

Cooking Tip: Be sure the broccoli is completely thawed before cooking to prevent it from watering out during baking.

3 tablespoons avocado oil, plus additional for greasing

1 (12-ounce) package 100% whole-wheat spaghetti

1 (8-ounce) package sliced fresh mushrooms

¼ cup 100% whole-wheat pastry flour

1 (14.5-ounce) can reduced-sodium chicken broth

1 cup milk

1 cup freshly grated Parmesan cheese

½ teaspoon salt

½ teaspoon freshly ground black pepper

1 (16-ounce) package frozen broccoli florets, thawed

2 cups shredded cooked chicken

1 cup sliced almonds

1. Preheat the oven to 400°F.
2. Coat a 13-by-9-inch baking dish with avocado oil.
3. Cook the pasta according to the package directions. Drain, and keep warm.
4. Heat 1 tablespoon of oil in a large nonstick skillet over medium heat. Add the mushrooms and cook 8 minutes or until browned and tender. Remove the mushrooms from the pan, and keep warm.
5. Heat the remaining 2 tablespoons of oil in the skillet. Whisk in the flour. Cook for 1 minute or until bubbling. Add the chicken broth. Bring to a boil and cook for 5 minutes or until thickened.
6. Stir in the milk, ½ cup of cheese, salt, and pepper. Cook for 1 more minute or until the cheese is melted.

continued ▶

7. In a large bowl, combine the pasta, mushrooms, cream sauce, broccoli, and chicken. Pour the mixture into prepared baking dish. Top evenly with the remaining ½ cup of cheese and almonds.
8. Bake for 25 to 30 minutes, until casserole is browned and bubbly.
9. Cut the tetrazzini into squares and serve.

Serves 6. Prep time: 20 minutes. Cooking time: 40 minutes. Total time: 1 hour.

....

Per serving: Calories: 377   Fat: 16g   Saturated Fat: 4.6g
Protein: 31.2g   Carbohydrates: 28.4g

Peanut Noodles with Shredded Pork and Vegetables

This simple noodle dish is a great way to reinvent leftover pork. If you don't have any leftover pork, shredded deli-roasted chicken is a perfect substitute. You can also make this dish as spicy as you'd like. If you're sensitive to heat, add less sambal oelek chili hot sauce, which is a great product to keep on hand, especially if you like spicy foods. You can find it in the international foods aisle.

Make-Ahead Tip: This simple dish is delicious hot or cold, making it an ideal make-ahead lunch. If you'd like to serve it warm, stir in a few tablespoons of hot water before serving. This dish will last for up to 2 days in the refrigerator.

8 ounces 100% whole-grain linguine

1 (16-ounce) package frozen stir-fry vegetables (no sauce)

½ cup Creamy Natural Peanut Butter (page 306)

2 tablespoons tamari or coconut aminos

2 garlic cloves, minced

1 tablespoon grated fresh ginger

1 teaspoon sambal oelek chili hot sauce (optional)

1 pound shredded cooked pork

¼ cup chopped fresh cilantro

Lime wedges

1. Cook the linguine according to the package directions; add the vegetables during the last minute of cooking. Drain, reserving 1 to 1½ cups of pasta water.
2. In a small bowl, whisk together the peanut butter, tamari, garlic, ginger, and hot sauce (if using). Return all the ingredients to the saucepan used for the pasta. Cook over medium heat for 4 minutes, adding enough pasta water to create a creamy sauce. Stir in the pork and cilantro.
3. Serve with lime wedges.

Serves 4. Prep time: 10 minutes. Cooking time: 20 minutes. Total Time: 30 minutes.

. . . .

Per serving: Calories: 605   Fat: 21.9g   Saturated Fat: 4.4g   Protein: 50.6g
Carbohydrates: 57.9g   Fiber: 10.9g

Stuffed Peppers

The addition of quinoa in this recipe adds extra protein and helps hold the stuffing mixture together. You may also try farro, barley, or brown rice for a variation. If you happen to have any cooked leftovers of any of these grains, that would be an added time-saver for making the dish.

½ cup uncooked quinoa

2 tablespoons avocado oil

1 onion, chopped

1 pound ground round beef

1 tablespoon chili powder

1 tablespoon tamari or
    coconut aminos

1 (14.5-ounce) can
    diced tomatoes

½ teaspoon salt

½ teaspoon freshly ground
    black pepper

6 red or green bell peppers,
    tops and seeds removed

1 cup shredded sharp white
    Cheddar cheese

⅓ cup water

1. Cook the quinoa according to the package directions; set aside.
2. Preheat the oven to 350°F.
3. Line a rimmed baking sheet with parchment paper.
4. In a large skillet over medium-high heat, heat the oil. Add the onion, beef, and chili powder. Cook for 8 minutes or until the beef is browned and the onion is tender. Drain.
5. In a large bowl, combine the quinoa, beef mixture, tamari, tomatoes, salt, and black pepper. Stuff the mixture into the bell peppers, dividing evenly.
6. Place the bell peppers on the prepared baking sheet. Top each with the cheese. Pour the water around the peppers in the bottom of the pan. Bake the peppers for 25 to 30 minutes or until the peppers are tender.
7. Remove the peppers from the oven and let rest for 5 to 10 minutes before serving.

Serves 6. Prep time: 15 minutes. Cooking time: 40 minutes.
Total time: 55 minutes (plus 5 minutes to rest).

. . . .

Per serving: Calories: 238   Fat: 11.1g   Saturated Fat: 5.2g   Protein: 13.4g
Carbohydrates: 21.6g   Fiber: 5.3g

Mini Meatloaves with Mashed Potatoes and Green Beans

Traditional meatloaf gets a modern update with these fun-to-eat meatloaf "muffins." Baking them in muffin tins helps save with cooking time and is a great built-in portion controller. If your kids aren't typically meatloaf eaters, this recipe just might change that.

Make-Ahead Tip: These meatloaf muffins can be made and frozen ahead. Try doubling the recipe and wrapping the uncooked meatloaf balls tightly in plastic wrap and freezing them in zip-top plastic bags for up to 1 month. Just thaw overnight in the refrigerator before baking as directed.

For the meatloaves:
Coconut oil, for greasing
1½ pounds ground
    round beef
1 egg, lightly beaten
½ cup finely chopped onion
¼ cup old-fashioned oats
3 tablespoons milk
1 tablespoon Italian seasoning
½ teaspoon salt
½ teaspoon freshly ground
    black pepper
¼ cup Spicy Chipotle Ketchup
    (page 290)

For the mashed potatoes:
1 pound new potatoes, cut into
    2-inch chunks
2 garlic cloves, minced
⅔ cup organic milk
½ teaspoon salt
½ teaspoon freshly ground
    black pepper
For the green beans:
3 cups frozen cut green beans
¼ teaspoon salt
¼ teaspoon freshly ground
    black pepper

To make the meatloaves:
1. Preheat the oven to 375°F.
2. Coat 8 cups of a muffin tin with coconut oil.

3. In a large bowl, mix together the beef, egg, onion, oats, milk, Italian seasoning, salt, and pepper. Let the mixture stand for 10 minutes.

4. Shape the mixture into 8 balls. Place the balls in the prepared muffin tin. Spread the ketchup evenly over the meatloaves. Place the muffin tin on a rimmed baking sheet.

5. Bake for 25 to 30 minutes or until the meatloaves reach 160°F; drain.

To make the mashed potatoes:

In a large Dutch oven over high heat, bring the potatoes and garlic to a boil. Cook for 15 to 20 minutes or until the potatoes are tender; drain. Mash the potatoes and garlic with a potato masher. Stir in the milk, salt, and pepper.

To make the green beans:

1. Place the green beans in a steamer basket in a medium saucepan over simmering water. Cover and cook for 5 minutes or until crisp-tender. Transfer the green beans to a serving bowl and sprinkle with the salt and pepper.

2. Serve the meatloaf muffins alongside the mashed potatoes and green beans.

Serves 4. Prep time: 20 minutes. Cooking time: 25 minutes.
Total time: 45 minutes (plus 10 minutes to stand).

....

Per serving: Calories: 300   Fat: 10g   Saturated Fat: 3.4g   Protein: 17.2g
Carbohydrates: 36g   Fiber: 6.8g

Maple-Sage Pork Tenderloin with Sautéed Mushroom Farro

This pork tenderloin with maple-mustard sauce, served with sautéed mushroom farro, is a delicious treat. This recipe calls for an oven-proof skillet to prevent dirtying more than one pan. A cast-iron skillet is a great option. If you don't have an oven-proof skillet, don't worry. You can easily transfer the pork to a baking pan after you brown it on the stove top.

Ingredient Tip: Packages of pork tenderloin usually include two tenderloins. For this recipe, buy a 3-pound package and use the other pork tenderloin for Pork and Peach Skewers with Grilled Asparagus (page 252). Or, wrap the extra tenderloin in plastic wrap, seal it tightly in a freezer bag, and freeze it for up to 1 month.

For the pork:
1½ pounds pork tenderloin
2 teaspoons dried sage
½ teaspoon salt
½ teaspoon pepper
2 tablespoons avocado oil
½ cup reduced-sodium
   chicken broth
¼ cup pure maple syrup
2 tablespoons apple
   cider vinegar
2 teaspoons grainy Dijon mustard

For the farro:
1 cup farro
2 tablespoons avocado oil
2 garlic cloves, minced
1 pound fresh
   mushrooms, sliced
½ teaspoon salt
½ teaspoon freshly ground
   black pepper

To make the pork:
1. Preheat the oven to 350°F.
2. Rub the pork tenderloin with sage, salt, and pepper.
3. Heat the oil in a cast-iron or oven-proof skillet over medium-high heat. Brown the pork on all sides, about 6 minutes.

4. Transfer the skillet to the oven and bake for 15 to 20 minutes, or until a thermometer registers 145°F.
5. Remove the pork from the skillet to a serving platter. Return the skillet to the stove top over medium heat.
6. Whisk together the chicken broth, maple syrup, vinegar, and mustard. Cook for 3 minutes or until the sauce is thick.
7. Slice the pork.

To make the farro:
1. Cook farro according to the package directions; keep warm.
2. Meanwhile, in a large nonstick skillet over medium-high heat, heat the oil. Add the garlic, mushrooms, salt, and pepper.
3. Cook for 10 minutes or until the mushrooms are browned and the liquid has evaporated. Stir in the farro.
4. Serve the sliced pork with the farro, spooned with sauce.

Serves 4. Prep time: 15 minutes. Cooking time: 25 minutes. Total time: 40 minutes.

. . . .

Per serving: Calories: 521   Fat: 9.4g   Saturated Fat: 2.5g   Protein: 56.1g
Carbohydrates: 53.9g   Fiber: 7.1g

Pork and Peach Skewers with Grilled Asparagus

Pork and summer-fresh peaches are a tasty pair. You can cook the pork kabobs and the asparagus on the grill at the same time. For ease in prepping, buy freestone peaches that release easily from the pit. If it's not summertime and you'd still like to make this recipe, you can often find peach slices in the frozen food aisle. And apple wedges are a good substitute for this dish.

Ingredient Tip: Did you know that thicker asparagus spears are actually more tender than pencil-thin? To ensure that the asparagus all cook at the same time, buy a bunch with evenly sized spears.

For the kabobs:

2 tablespoons apple
   cider vinegar

½ cup honey

½ cup Dijon mustard

1 teaspoon dried thyme

1½ pounds pork tenderloin, cut
   into 1-inch cubes

3 peaches, cut into wedges

1 onion, cut into wedges

For the asparagus:

1½ pounds asparagus, trimmed

2 tablespoons avocado oil

½ teaspoon salt

½ teaspoon freshly ground
   black pepper

To make the kabobs:

1. Preheat the grill to medium-high heat.
2. In a small bowl, whisk together the vinegar, honey, mustard, and thyme. Set aside.
3. Thread the pork, peaches, and onion alternately onto 8 (10-inch) metal skewers. Brush the kabobs with half of the glaze mixture.
4. Grill the kabobs for 5 minutes on each side, or until the pork is done, basting with remaining glaze while grilling.

To make the asparagus:

1. In a large bowl, toss together the asparagus, oil, salt and pepper.
2. Grill the asparagus for 8 minutes, turning occasionally, or until it is crisp-tender.
3. Serve the kabobs on the skewers with the asparagus on the side.

Serves 4. Prep time: 20 minutes. Cooking time: 10 minutes. Total time: 30 minutes.

. . . .

Per serving: Calories: 480   Fat: 8.5g   Saturated Fat: 2.4g   Protein: 50.8g
Carbohydrates: 53.5g   Fiber: 6.8g

Shredded Beef Tacos

This dinner is a lifesaver on weeknights when schedules are full. The recipe calls for cooked beef, which you may have on hand from dishes like Slow-Cooked Italian Pot Roast and Vegetables (page 258), if you're moving through the meal plan. If you don't have any leftover beef, or would like a different take on tacos, you can substitute shredded pork or chicken.

Serving Tip: Make it a Mexican party and create a taco topping bar for everyone to dress their tacos as they'd like. Fill all sorts of small serving bowls with vegetables, sour cream, black beans, chopped romaine lettuce, chopped black olives, shredded sharp white Cheddar cheese, Fresh Salsa (page 297), etc.

2 tablespoons avocado oil

½ cup chopped onion

1 garlic clove, minced

1 teaspoon chili powder

½ teaspoon ground cumin

4 cups shredded cooked beef

¼ cup reduced-sodium
   beef broth

1 cup Chunky Guacamole
   (page 300)

8 (6-inch) 100% whole-wheat
   tortillas, warmed

2 large tomatoes, diced

2 tablespoons chopped
   fresh cilantro

1. In a large skillet over medium heat, heat the oil; add the onion and garlic. Sauté for 5 minutes or until the onion is tender. Stir in the chili powder, cumin, beef, and broth. Cook for 5 minutes or until the beef is heated.
2. Spoon the guacamole onto the tortillas, dividing evenly. Top the guacamole with the beef mixture, tomatoes, and cilantro. Serve.

Serves 4. Prep time: 10 minutes. Cooking time: 10 minutes. Total time: 20 minutes.

Per serving: Calories: 399   Fat: 17.5g   Saturated Fat: 4.5g   Protein: 30.6g
Carbohydrates: 31.6g   Fiber: 8.2g

Steak with Onion-Mushroom Sauce

This tenderloin steak recipe is a special-occasion dish, perfect for a romantic date night at home or for celebrating a birthday. The simple mushroom-onion sauce is infused with fresh thyme and is oh so good served over mashed potatoes alongside steamed green beans.

Ingredient Tip: Some grocery stores sell beef tenderloin tails at a much lower price than beef tenderloin steaks. These are the smaller ends of the beef tenderloin that are often hard to sell, but they are the same cut of beef and taste just as delicious.

2 (4-ounce) beef
   tenderloin steaks
½ teaspoon salt
½ teaspoon freshly ground
   black pepper
1 tablespoon avocado oil
1 small onion, sliced

1 (8-ounce) package sliced
   fresh mushrooms
1 teaspoon fresh thyme
¾ cup reduced-sodium
   beef broth
2 teaspoons arrowroot powder

1. Sprinkle the steaks with salt and pepper.
2. In a skillet over medium-high heat, heat the oil. Add the steaks and cook for 3 to 4 minutes on each side or to desired doneness. Remove the steaks from the pan and keep warm.
3. Reduce heat to medium. Add the onion and mushrooms to the pan. Cook for 10 minutes or until the mushrooms are tender.
4. In a small bowl, whisk together the thyme, broth, and arrowroot powder. Add the mixture to the pan. Cook, stirring constantly, for 2 minutes or until the sauce is thickened.
5. Spoon the sauce over the steaks to serve.

Serves 2. Prep time: 10 minutes. Cooking time: 15 minutes. Total time: 25 minutes.

. . . .

Per serving: Calories: 274   Fat: 8.3g   Saturated Fat: 2.9g   Protein: 38.4g
Carbohydrates: 10.7g   Fiber: 2.5g

Sausage, Lentil, and Kale Stew

Gluten-Free
Dairy-Free

This comforting, healthy soup can easily be served as a vegetarian dish. Omit the sausage and add a little extra avocado oil. Leftovers also make a great lunch for the following day. Or, make a double batch and freeze leftovers for an on-hand dinner you can heat up quickly in a pinch.

Time-Saving Tip: Kale is readily available pre-washed and pre-chopped in 1-pound bags at the grocery store. You can use it in this soup to help save on prep time.

2 tablespoons avocado oil

1 pound lean Italian turkey
    sausage, casings removed

1 onion, chopped

2 garlic cloves, minced

1 teaspoon dried oregano

8 ounces dried brown
    lentils, rinsed

4 cups reduced-sodium
    chicken broth

3 cups water

1 pound fresh kale,
    coarsely chopped

½ teaspoon salt

½ teaspoon freshly ground
    black pepper

1. In a large Dutch oven over medium-high heat, heat the oil. Add the sausage and cook until browned and crumbled, about 5 minutes. Remove the sausage with a slotted spoon, reserving the drippings in the pan.
2. Add the onion and garlic to the pan. Cook for 5 minutes or until the onion is tender.
3. Add the oregano, lentils, broth, and 3 cups water. Bring to a boil; reduce the heat, and simmer for 25 to 30 minutes or until the lentils are tender.
4. Stir in the kale, sausage, salt, and pepper. Cover and cook for 5 more minutes or until the kale is wilted and the stew is very hot.

Serves 4. Prep time: 10 minutes. Cooking time: 40 minutes. Total time: 50 minutes.

....

Per serving: Calories: 461 Fat: 13.6g Saturated Fat: 3.3g Protein: 39.4g
Carbohydrates: 44.4g Fiber: 7.9g

Slow-Cooked Italian Pot Roast and Vegetables

Enjoy slow-cooked pot roast any night of the week with this quick-to-prep recipe. Start the roast first thing in the morning before work or a day of errands, and come home to a comforting meal.

Cooking Tip: Browning the roast first before putting it in the slow cooker locks in the flavorful juices and adds extra flavor.

2 (2-pound) eye-of-round beef roasts

1 teaspoon salt

1 teaspoon freshly ground black pepper

1 tablespoon coconut oil

½ pound carrots, peeled and cut into 2-inch chunks

2 sweet potatoes, peeled and cut into 2-inch chunks

½ pound new potatoes, halved

1 onion, chopped

4 garlic cloves, minced

1 (14.5-ounce) can diced tomatoes

1 (14.5-ounce) can reduced-sodium beef broth

3 tablespoons water

3 tablespoons arrowroot powder

1. Rub the roast evenly with salt and pepper.
2. Heat the oil in a Dutch oven over medium-high heat. Brown the roast on all sides, about 10 minutes. Transfer the roast to a 5- to 6-quart slow cooker.
3. Add the carrots, sweet potatoes, new potatoes, onion, garlic, tomatoes, and beef broth to the slow cooker.
4. Cover and cook on low for 8 hours or until the roast is tender. Remove the roast and vegetables from the slow cooker.
5. In a small bowl, whisk together the water and arrowroot powder. Add the mixture to the juices in the slow cooker. Cook, uncovered, on high for 5 minutes or until thickened.
6. Serve the beef and vegetables drizzled with the sauce.

Serves 10. Prep time: 20 minutes. Cooking time: 8 hours, 15 minutes. Total time: 8 hours, 35 minutes.

. . . .

Per serving: Calories: 425 Fat: 9.6g Saturated Fat: 4.4g Protein: 50.7g Carbohydrates: 30.5g Fiber: 3.8g

Grilled Flank Steak with Cucumber, Tomato, and Corn Relish

Gluten-Free
Dairy-Free

This dish captures all of the fresh flavors of summer. Crunchy cucumbers and juicy tomatoes in the relish are the perfect complement to the spice-rubbed steak.

2 pounds flank steak

2 garlic cloves, minced

1 tablespoon chili powder

1 teaspoon salt

½ teaspoon freshly ground black pepper

2 ears corn, shucked and cleaned

2 tomatoes, diced

1 cucumber, diced

½ cup finely chopped onion

3 tablespoons extra-virgin olive oil

2 tablespoons lemon juice

¼ cup chopped fresh basil

2 tablespoons chopped fresh mint

1. Preheat the grill to medium-high heat.
2. Rub the flank steak with the minced garlic, chili powder, ¾ teaspoon of salt, and ¼ teaspoon of pepper. Grill the steak, covered with the grill lid, for 6 to 7 minutes on each side or to desired degree of doneness. Let the steak rest for 10 minutes before thinly slicing against the grain.
3. While the steak grills, cut the tips off the corn. Stand an ear in a wide shallow bowl and cut off the kernels; use the back of the knife to scrape the pulp from the corn cobs. Repeat with each ear. In a large bowl, combine the corn, tomatoes, cucumber, onion, remaining ¼ teaspoon of salt, remaining ¼ teaspoon of pepper, olive oil, lemon juice, basil, and mint.
4. Serve the relish with the sliced steak.

Serves 6. Prep time: 15 minutes. Cooking time: 15 minutes.
Total time: 30 minutes (plus 10 minutes to stand).

. . . .

Per serving: Calories: 400 Fat: 20.2g Saturated Fat: 6.3g Protein: 43.8g
Carbohydrates: 10.5g Fiber: 2.2g

Shepherd's Pie

Shepherd's pie is traditional British pub food. Red-skinned new potatoes are a great choice of potatoes for this dish. They are filled with healthy vitamins and nutrients, and are a great source of fiber and vitamin B_6. Because most of the nutritional value is found in a potato's skin, leave the peel on, you won't want to peel the potatoes.

Serving Tip: Make individual shepherd's pies and keep some frozen to thaw and bake on busy nights. To do this, spoon the filling into 10-ounce ramekins and top with the mashed potatoes. Cover the pies with plastic wrap and freeze them for 24 hours. Once frozen, remove the ramekins from the freezer and run a bit of warm water over the bottom to help pop out the pies. Wrap individual pies in tin foil and return them to the freezer for up to 1 month. When ready to eat, allow them to thaw, then bake as directed.

1 pound new potatoes, cut into 2-inch chunks

2 garlic cloves, minced

2/3 cup milk

1 teaspoon salt

1 teaspoon freshly ground black pepper

2 tablespoons avocado oil

1 onion, chopped

1 pound ground round beef

1½ cups frozen peas and carrots, thawed

1 cup reduced-sodium beef broth

1 tablespoon tomato paste

1 tablespoon tamari or coconut aminos

1. Preheat the oven to 375°F.

2. In a large Dutch oven over high heat, bring the potatoes and garlic to a boil. Cook for 15 to 20 minutes or until the potatoes are tender; drain. Mash the potatoes and garlic with a potato masher. Stir in the milk and ½ teaspoon each of salt and pepper. Set aside.

3. While the potatoes cook, in a large nonstick skillet over medium-high heat, heat the oil. Add the onion and beef. Cook for 8 minutes or until the beef is no longer pink and the onion is tender; drain and discard the fat.

4. Add the peas and carrots to the beef mixture. Cook for 3 minutes or until hot.
5. In a medium bowl, whisk together the beef broth, tomato paste, tamari, and remaining salt and pepper. Pour the mixture over the beef, and stir to combine. Cook for 3 more minutes or until the liquid is absorbed.
6. Spoon the beef mixture into an 11-by-7-inch baking dish. Spoon the mashed potatoes over the beef mixture in an even layer. Use a fork to make a crosshatch design.
7. Bake for 30 minutes or until the potatoes are golden brown and filling is bubbly. Let stand for 5 minutes before serving.
8. Serve hot.

Serves 6. Prep time: 10 minutes. Cooking time: 45 minutes.
Total time: 55 minutes (plus 5 minutes to stand).

. . . .

Per serving: Calories: 206   Fat: 4.8g   Saturated Fat: 1.6g   Protein: 12.6g
Carbohydrates: 31.4g   Fiber: 7.2g

11

Dessert

Amaretti Cookies

With only five ingredients and 15 minutes of hands-on time, it's easy to see why these Italian cookies are so popular. The sweet almond flavor and crispy texture make them the tasty treat to dip into tea, coffee, or hot chocolate. And they remain fresh for up to 1 week stored in an airtight container, if they last that long.

Make-Ahead Tip: Since this recipe makes 18 cookies, you may want to freeze half of the dough to use later, especially if they're part of your meal plan. Simply wrap it tightly in plastic wrap and store it in a resealable bag in the freezer for up to 1 month. Thaw it completely before dropping the batter into mounds and baking.

3 egg whites, at room
   temperature
¾ cup almond flour

¾ cup coconut sugar
½ teaspoon almond extract
Sliced almonds, optional

1. Preheat the oven to 350°F.
2. Line a baking sheet with parchment paper.
3. In a medium bowl, stir together the egg whites, almond flour, sugar, and almond extract. Drop the batter by the teaspoon onto the baking sheet, leaving 2 inches between each mound. Top each mound with 1 almond slice (if using).
4. Bake, in 2 batches, for 12 to 15 minutes or until the edges are golden brown and the centers are just set. Transfer the cookies to cooling racks to cool (cookies will crisp up as they cool).
5. Serve or store the cookies in an airtight container for up to 1 week.

Makes 18 cookies. Prep time: 15 minutes. Cooking time: 15 minutes. Total time: 30 minutes.

. . . .

Per serving (1 cookie):   Calories: 63   Fat: 2.5g   Saturated Fat: 0g
Protein: 0.6g   Carbohydrates: 8.9g   Fiber: 0.5g

Lemon-Lime Granita

Vegan
Gluten-Free

This tart and tangy treat is a refreshing way to finish a meal. It's easy to make ahead and keep in the freezer for times when you need something sweet. Try experimenting with other fresh juices for a new twist to this elegant, traditional Italian dessert.

Cooking Tip: Freezing this dessert in a metal baking dish helps it freeze evenly and quickly.

¼ cup fresh lemon juice

¼ cup fresh lime juice

1 cup water

¼ cup liquid stevia

1 teaspoon fresh lemon zest

1 teaspoon fresh lemon rind

1. Combine the lemon juice, lime juice, water, stevia, lemon zest, and lime rind in a shallow metal baking dish. Stir well, then place the dish in the freezer.
2. Stir the mixture with a fork every 10 to 15 minutes until it becomes slushy, about 45 minutes.
3. Once the granita is slushy, leave it in the freezer and scrape it around every 10 minutes until it has a crystalized, icy texture.
4. Spoon the granita into dessert cups and serve immediately.

Serves 4. Prep time: 1 hour.

. . . .

Per serving: Calories: 72   Fat: 0.1g   Saturated Fat: 0g   Protein: 0.3g
Carbohydrates: 19.1g   Fiber: 0g

Broiled Grapefruit with Honeyed Yogurt

This simple, elegant, unusual dessert is even great for breakfast sprinkled with some wholesome granola. Whether for dessert or for breakfast, it is sure to be a big hit. Ruby red grapefruits tend to be sweeter than yellow grapefruits and are at their peak during winter months.

Cooking Tip: Prevent your grapefruits from wiggling around in the baking pan by cutting a small slice off the bottoms to steady them.

3 ruby red grapefruits, halved and cut along the segments

6 tablespoons coconut sugar

¼ teaspoon ground cinnamon

½ cup plain Greek yogurt

3 tablespoons honey

1. Preheat the broiler to high.
2. Place the grapefruit halves, cut-side up, in a 13-by-9-inch baking pan. Sprinkle the grapefruit with coconut sugar and cinnamon.
3. Broil for 5 minutes or until the sugar is caramelized. Watch carefully so they don't burn. Remove to a wire rack to cool a bit.
4. Meanwhile, in a small bowl, stir together the yogurt and honey. Dollop it evenly on warm grapefruit halves.
5. Serve warm.

Serves 6. Prep time: 5 minutes. Cooking time: 5 minutes. Total time: 10 minutes.

. . . .

Per serving: Calories: 115   Fat: 0.9g   Saturated Fat: 0.5g   Protein: 2g
Carbohydrates: 26.7g   Fiber: 0.8g

Frozen Blueberry-Granola Bars

These frozen treats are the perfect ending to a hot day with a creamy, tart filling and crunchy granola crust. If you want to trade out home-made granola for store-bought, look for 100% whole-grain granola without any hidden sugars.

Storage Tip: A metal baking pan is the right choice for this dessert. Choose one that is heavy-duty, and cover it with plastic wrap before freezing.

1 cup Spiced Pecan-Almond
   Granola with Dried Fruit
   (page 138)
2 cups fresh blueberries
3 cups plain Greek yogurt

⅓ cup honey
1 teaspoon grated fresh
   lemon zest
½ teaspoon almond extract

1. Line an 8-inch-square baking pan with aluminum foil. Spread the granola in an even layer in the bottom of the pan.
2. In a blender or food processor, blend the blueberries, yogurt, honey, lemon zest, and almond extract until smooth. Pour the blueberry mixture over the granola in the pan, spreading it in an even layer.
3. Cover and freeze for 4 hours, or until firm. Keep frozen until ready to serve.
4. Warm a knife under hot water, dry it, and cut the frozen granola bars to serve.

Serves 8. Prep time: 15 minutes. Total time: 15 minutes (plus 4 hours to freeze).
. . . .
Per serving: Calories: 136   Fat: 11.2g   Saturated Fat: 3.5g   Protein: 12g
Carbohydrates: 25.5g   Fiber: 3.6g

Strawberry Shortcakes

Sweet and tender, these shortcakes make the perfect nest for juicy strawberries. Crowned with a dollop of sweetened yogurt, this dessert will satisfy every craving.

Ingredient Variation: These shortcakes are great with other sliced fruit as well. Try them with sliced peaches, mango, plums, or even fresh berries.

1 cup 100% whole-wheat
    pastry flour
2 tablespoons coconut sugar
1 teaspoon baking powder
¼ teaspoon salt
2 tablespoons cold butter, cut
    into small pieces

1 egg
½ teaspoon pure vanilla extract
¼ cup milk
2 cups sliced fresh strawberries
1 cup plain Greek yogurt
2 tablespoons honey

1. Preheat the oven to 375°F.
2. Line a rimmed baking sheet with parchment paper.
3. In a large bowl, whisk together the flour, sugar, baking powder, and salt. Cut the butter in using a pastry blender or two forks until the mixture resembles coarse crumbs.
4. In a separate bowl, whisk together the egg, vanilla extract, and milk. Add the wet ingredients to the flour mixture, mixing just until the dough comes together. Transfer the dough to the prepared pan and press to ½ inch thickness. Bake for 15 minutes or until a toothpick inserted in the center comes out clean. Transfer the shortcake to a wire rack to cool.
5. Cut the shortcake into 4 pieces; split each in half crosswise. Top evenly with strawberries.
6. In a small bowl, stir together the yogurt and honey. Spoon the mixture evenly on four pieces. Top the mixture with the remaining halves and serve.

Serves 4. Prep time: 15 minutes. Cooking time: 15 minutes. Total time: 30 minutes.

Per serving: Calories: 256 Fat: 10.1g Saturated Fat: 5.7g Protein: 9.2g Carbohydrates: 34.2g Fiber: 2.5g

Vegetarian

Apple Crumble

Reminiscent of the apple pie grandma used to make, this crumble is a comforting classic. And it's full of healthy benefits. Apples are a great source of fiber, vitamin C, and antioxidants, and one a day surely enhances your health.

Cooking Tip: Don't let the butter get too soft before making the crumble topping. It should still be firm to help give the topping structure during baking.

Coconut oil, for greasing
4 apples, peeled and
    thinly sliced
3 tablespoons lemon juice
½ teaspoon pure
    vanilla extract
4 tablespoons evaporated
    cane juice
1 teaspoon ground cinnamon

¼ teaspoon ground nutmeg
7 tablespoons 100% whole-
    wheat pastry flour
½ cup uncooked old-fashioned
    rolled oats
¼ cup chopped almonds
2 tablespoons cold butter,
    cut into pieces

1. Preheat the oven to 375°F.
2. Coat an 8-inch-square baking pan with coconut oil.
3. In a medium bowl, toss together the apples, lemon juice, vanilla, 1 tablespoon of evaporated cane juice, ½ teaspoon of cinnamon, nutmeg, and 1 tablespoon of flour. Pour the mixture into the prepared baking pan.
4. In a separate medium bowl, stir together the remaining 6 table-spoons of flour, oats, the remaining ½ teaspoon of cinnamon, the remaining 3 tablespoons of cane juice, almonds, and butter; mix with a fork or fingers until crumbly. Spoon the crumble mixture evenly over the apples.
5. Bake for 20 to 25 minutes or until the topping is golden and the apples are juicy and fork-tender. Serve warm.

Serves 6. Prep time: 10 minutes. Cooking time: 20 minutes. Total time: 30 minutes.

Per serving: Calories: 167   Fat: 6.5g   Saturated Fat: 2.6g   Protein: 2.5g
Carbohydrates: 26.9g   Fiber: 4.9g

Apple-Raisin Rice Pudding

Rice pudding is the ultimate kid-friendly treat. Its creamy texture and vanilla flavoring can be matched by no other dessert. It's important to use short-grain rice in this recipe to attain the perfect smoothness to the pudding. Stove top-simmered rice pudding, like this recipe, involves a lot of stirring but that makes it creamy and memorable.

Make-Ahead Tip: Make this rice pudding ahead of time and keep it in the refrigerator for an easy dessert during the week. You can serve it warm or chilled.

3 cups milk	**¼ cup dried apples**
½ cup short-grain brown rice	**Pinch salt**
¼ cup pure maple syrup	**1 teaspoon pure vanilla extract**
¼ cup raisins	**1 teaspoon ground cinnamon**

1. In a medium saucepan, combine the milk, rice, maple syrup, raisins, apples, and salt. Bring to a boil, stirring frequently to prevent scorching.
2. Reduce the heat to low and simmer, uncovered, for 20 to 25 minutes, stirring frequently until the rice is tender and the mixture is creamy.
3. Stir in the vanilla and cinnamon. Serve warm or cover and refrigerate up to 1 week.

Serves 4. Prep time: 30 minutes. Cooking time: 40 minutes.
Total time: 1 hour, 10 minutes.

. . . .

Per serving: Calories: 264   Fat: 4.5g   Saturated Fat: 2.4g   Protein: 8.1g
Carbohydrates: 49g   Fiber: 1.6g

Carrot Cake Cupcakes

Cupcakes are quite possibly the world's best dessert, and these tasty treats will be loved by both kids and adults alike. For a special touch, sprinkle chopped toasted walnuts on the frosting. Be sure to shred your own carrots instead of buying them already prepared at the store—pre-shredded carrots are dried out and will lend a dry texture to the cupcakes.

Storage Tip: Keep these tender treats stored in an airtight container in the refrigerator for up to 4 days.

For the cupcakes:

1¼ cup 100% whole-wheat pastry flour

1 teaspoon baking powder

1 teaspoon ground cinnamon

½ teaspoon ground ginger

¼ teaspoon ground cloves

¼ teaspoon baking soda

¼ teaspoon salt

2 eggs

⅔ cup coconut sugar

½ cup coconut oil

1½ cups grated carrot (about 3 large carrots)

½ cup finely chopped walnuts

For the frosting:

1 (8-ounce) package cream cheese, at room temperature

3 tablespoons maple syrup

1 teaspoon pure vanilla extract

To make the cupcakes:

1. Preheat the oven to 325°F.
2. Place paper liners in 12 cups of a standard muffin tin.
3. In a medium bowl, whisk together the flour, baking powder, cinnamon, ginger, cloves, baking soda, and salt. Set aside.
4. In the bowl of a mixer, beat the eggs, sugar, and oil. Add the flour mixture, stirring just until moistened. Stir in carrots and walnuts.
5. Spoon the batter evenly into the muffin tin. Bake for 18 to 20 minutes or until a toothpick inserted in the center comes out clean.
6. Remove the cupcakes from the tin and cool completely on a wire rack, about 15 minutes.

To make the frosting:

1. In a medium bowl, beat the cream cheese with an electric mixer until creamy. Add the maple syrup and vanilla extract; beat until combined.
2. Spread the frosting onto the cooled cupcakes.
3. Store leftover cupcakes in an airtight container for up to 3 days at room temperature.

Makes 12. Prep time: 15 minutes. Cooking time: 20 minutes.
Total time: 35 minutes (plus 15 minutes to cool).

. . . .

Per serving (1 cupcake):   Calories: 293   Fat: 19.7g   Saturated Fat: 12.4g   Protein: 5.6g
Carbohydrates: 26.2g   Fiber: 1.8g

Yogurt Cheesecake Bars with Berry Topping

These tart and creamy bars are a healthier version of classic cheesecake. The berry sauce is a scrumptious addition and makes these a dessert worthy of a special occasion.

Cooking Tip: Don't overbeat the cream cheese filling; doing so introduces air to the batter, which in turn can cause it to crack during baking.

Coconut oil, for greasing
¾ cup uncooked old-fashioned rolled oats
¼ cup almond flour
1 teaspoon ground cinnamon
4½ tablespoons coconut sugar
1½ tablespoons butter, melted
1½ tablespoons unsweetened almond milk

1 (8-ounce) package cream cheese, softened
¼ cup honey
2 eggs
1 tablespoon pure vanilla extract
1 teaspoon lemon zest
1 cup plain Greek yogurt
1 cup Warm Berry Sauce (page 308)

1. Preheat the oven to 325°F.
2. Coat an 8-inch-square pan with coconut oil.
3. In a food processor, pulse the oats, almond flour, cinnamon, and 2½ tablespoons of coconut sugar until coarsely ground. Add the butter and milk; pulse until the mixture resembles wet crumbs. Press the crust into the prepared pan. Bake for 8 minutes or until set; let cool slightly.
4. In a large bowl, beat the cream cheese, honey, and remaining 2 tablespoons coconut sugar with a mixer at medium speed until fluffy. Add the eggs, one at a time, beating until the yellow disappears. Add the vanilla, lemon zest, and yogurt and beat just until combined. Pour the filling over the prepared crust. Bake for 30 to 35 minutes or until the center jiggles slightly.

5. Remove the cheesecake from the oven and cool completely. Refrigerate the cheesecake for 3 hours or until chilled; cut into squares.

6. Serve with the sauce spooned over the squares.

Serves 8. Prep time: 20 minutes. Cooking time: 40 minutes.
Total time: 1 hour (plus 3 hours to chill).

. . . .

Per serving: Calories: 379   Fat: 22.9g   Saturated Fat: 12.5g   Protein: 7.3g
Carbohydrates: 36.6g   Fiber: 2.7g

Quick Vanilla Pudding

Vegetarian
Gluten-Free

This simple pudding gets its thickness from arrowroot powder and egg yolk. To make it have intense vanilla flavor, rather than using vanilla extract, scrape the seeds from a vanilla bean into the milk mixture before it thickens.

Serving Tip: If you don't want to wait for the pudding to get cold, you can eat it warm. It serves as the perfect blank palette for stirring in bittersweet chocolate or fresh fruit.

2 tablespoons
   arrowroot powder
2 cups milk
2 tablespoons evaporated
   cane juice

1 tablespoon pure
   vanilla extract
1 egg yolk
1 cup fresh raspberries, for
   garnish

1. In a medium saucepan, whisk together the arrowroot and milk until no lumps remain; whisk in the cane juice and vanilla extract. Bring the mixture to a simmer over medium heat. Cook for 1 to 2 minutes, whisking constantly until thickened.
2. Place the egg yolk in a small bowl. Add 1 tablespoon of the hot milk mixture, whisking constantly so the egg yolk doesn't cook. Add another 1 tablespoon of hot milk mixture and whisk again. Then, whisking constantly, pour the milk–egg yolk mixture into the thickened hot milk. Cook for 1 more minute or until thickened.
3. Divide the pudding among dessert dishes and refrigerate until set, at least 1 hour. Serve chilled, garnished with fresh raspberries.

Serves 4. Prep time: 5 minutes. Cooking time: 5 minutes.
Total time: 10 minutes (plus 1 hour to chill).

. . . .

Per serving: Calories: 122 Fat: 3.8g Saturated Fat: 1.9g Protein: 5g
Carbohydrates: 15.7g Fiber: 2g

Chocolate-Dipped Peppermint Meringues

These crispy cookies are only 14 calories each, and they're just the ticket to satisfying your sweet tooth. For a fun twist, sprinkle crushed peppermints onto the chocolate before it dries. It'll make the perfect gift for the holidays.

Cooking Tip: Wait to add the peppermint extract until after the egg whites are beaten to stiff peaks. Peppermint extract usually contains peppermint oil, which will prevent the egg whites from forming stiff peaks if you add it too soon.

3 egg whites

¼ teaspoon cream of tartar

3 tablespoons pure maple syrup

¼ teaspoon pure peppermint extract

4 ounces 70% bittersweet chocolate, chopped

1. Preheat the oven to 250°F.
2. Line rimmed baking sheets with parchment paper.
3. In a mixer, beat the egg whites and cream of tartar to soft peaks. Add the maple syrup and beat until stiff peaks form. Gently fold in the peppermint extract.
4. Transfer the mixture to a pastry bag fitted with a ½-inch tip. Pipe the mixture onto the prepared baking sheet to 1-inch rounds.
5. Bake for 35 to 40 minutes or until dry. Remove the cookies from the oven and let them cool completely on the pan.
6. Place the chocolate in a small bowl over a saucepan of simmering water. Cook for 5 minutes, or until the chocolate is melted, stirring frequently.

7. Dip each meringue halfway into the chocolate. Let cool on the parchment.
8. Store the meringues in an airtight container at room temperature for up to 2 weeks.

Makes 5 dozen. Prep time: 20 minutes. Cooking time: 40 minutes. Total time: 1 hour.

. . . .

Per serving (1 cookie):   Calories: 14   Fat: 0.6g   Saturated Fat: 0g   Protein: 0.3g
Carbohydrates: 1.8g   Fiber: 0g

Dark Cherry, Pistachio, Coconut, and Bittersweet Chocolate Bark

When you are craving chocolate, this gourmet treat is sure to satisfy. Bedecked with vibrant green pistachios, tart dried cherries, toasted coconut, and a hint of saltiness, your taste buds will thank you. This sweet but healthy treat is best served chilled, and it makes a great gift.

Cooking Tip: A double boiler is a sure-fire way to protect the chocolate from becoming scorched. Be sure to stir the chocolate constantly as it melts to prevent hot spots.

12 ounces 70% bittersweet chocolate, chopped

1 cup coarsely chopped unsalted shelled pistachios

1 cup dried unsweetened cherries

¼ cup shredded unsweetened coconut, toasted

½ teaspoon coarse sea salt

1. Line a rimmed baking sheet with parchment paper.
2. In a medium bowl over a saucepan of simmering water, melt the chocolate, stirring frequently, until smooth and melted, about 5 minutes.
3. Pour the melted chocolate onto the prepared baking sheet, spreading it to about ¼ inch thickness. Sprinkle evenly with the pistachios, cherries, coconut, and salt.
4. Chill until the bark is firm, about 30 minutes. Peel off the parchment paper and break the chocolate into pieces.
5. Store the bark in the refrigerator in an airtight container for up to 1 month.

Serves 16. Prep time: 5 minutes. Cooking time: 5 minutes. Total time: 10 minutes (plus 30 minutes to chill).

Per serving: Calories: 185   Fat: 10.3g   Saturated Fat: 5.2g   Protein: 3.8g   Carbohydrates: 21.6g   Fiber: 2.4g

Dark Chocolate Bread Puddings

Baking these little bread puddings in individual muffin cups is great for portion control and for storing. You can just as easily bake these in a 13-by-9-inch baking dish, or in small ramekins for an elegant look. If you use a large baking dish, add an extra 15 to 20 minutes to the baking time.

Storage Tip: Wrap any leftover bread puddings in plastic wrap and keep them refrigerated for up to 3 days. You can serve them cold or zap them in the microwave for 10 seconds to melt the chocolate.

Coconut oil, for greasing

3 cups milk

4 eggs, lightly beaten

¾ cup evaporated cane juice

2 tablespoons unsweetened cocoa powder

½ teaspoon pure vanilla extract

12 ounces 100% whole-grain bread, cut into 1-inch pieces

8 ounces 70% bittersweet chocolate, chopped

1. Preheat the oven to 350°F.
2. Coat 12 cups of a standard muffin tin with coconut oil.
3. In a large bowl, whisk together the milk, eggs, cane juice, cocoa powder, and vanilla. Add the bread and chocolate. Let stand for 10 minutes.
4. Fill the prepared muffin tin with the bread mixture. Bake for 25 minutes, or until set.
5. Serve warm, or cool and refrigerate, covered, for 3 days.

Serves 12. Prep time: 15 minutes. Cooking time: 25 minutes.
Total time: 40 minutes (plus 10 minutes to stand).

. . . .

Per serving: Calories: 227   Fat: 9.6g   Saturated Fat: 5.2g   Protein: 8.7g
Carbohydrates: 27g   Fiber: 4.1g

Fudgy Chocolate Chunk– Pecan Brownies

If you are a chocoholic, this is the dessert for you. Chewy, rich brownies are studded with chunks of dark chocolate and toasty pecans. It's the perfect treat to take with you on the go or to enjoy at the end of a long day.

Double It: These brownies are perfect to bake and take to a potluck or to feed a crowd. Double the ingredients and bake in a 13-by-9-inch baking pan. Add 2 to 5 minutes to the baking time. Or if the brownies are a dessert on your meal plan, freeze them and defrost for 3 to 4 hours in plastic wrap at room temperature before eating.

Coconut oil, for greasing

½ cup butter, melted

1 cup coconut sugar

1 teaspoon pure vanilla extract

2 eggs

⅓ cup unsweetened
  cocoa powder

½ cup 100% whole-wheat
  pastry flour

¼ teaspoon baking powder

¼ teaspoon salt

½ cup chopped 70%
  bittersweet chocolate

½ cup chopped
  pecans, toasted

1. Preheat the oven to 350°F.
2. Coat a 9-inch-square baking pan with coconut oil.
3. In a medium bowl, stir together the butter, sugar, vanilla extract, and eggs. In a separate medium bowl, whisk together the cocoa powder, pastry flour, baking powder, salt, chocolate, and pecans. Add the dry mixture to the butter mixture, stirring just until combined. (The batter will be thick.)
4. Spread the batter into the prepared pan. Bake for 18 to 20 minutes or until set. Serve warm or at room temperature.

Serves 12. Prep time: 10 minutes. Cooking time: 20 minutes. Total time: 30 minutes.

. . . .

Per serving: Calories: 199   Fat: 11.7g   Saturated Fat: 6.8g   Protein: 2.5g
Carbohydrates: 23.5g   Fiber: 1.3g

Coconut Cream Pie

This is a special dessert and will probably be requested often in your house. A quick almond flour crust is topped by creamy and sweet coconut filling and garnished with toasted coconut. For an even more decadent treat, dollop Coconut Whipped Cream (page 310) over the top before garnishing with the toasted coconut.

Cooking Tip: Arrowroot can be sensitive, so be sure to cook the mixture just until the filling thickens and then remove it from the heat. Otherwise, the sauce may break down and thin out.

For the crust:
¾ cup almond flour
1 tablespoon evaporated cane juice
3 tablespoons butter, melted
For the filling:
1 (13.5-ounce) can coconut milk
1 egg
3 tablespoons arrowroot powder

3 tablespoons evaporated cane juice
Pinch salt
1 teaspoon pure vanilla extract
½ cup unsweetened shredded coconut
Toasted unsweetened shredded coconut, for sprinkling

To make the crust:
1. Preheat the oven to 350°F.
2. In a small bowl, stir together the flour, cane juice, and butter. Press the crust into a 9-inch pie plate.
3. Bake for 10 minutes or until the crust is golden brown. Remove the crust from the oven and let cool.

To make the filling:
1. In a medium saucepan, combine the coconut milk, egg, arrowroot powder, cane juice, and salt.
2. Bring the mixture to a simmer, stirring constantly until it thickens, about 5 minutes.
3. Stir in the vanilla and shredded coconut.

4. Pour the filling into the prepared crust. Cover and refrigerate for 4 hours or until firm.

5. Sprinkle the pie with the toasted coconut before serving.

Serves 8. Prep time: 15 minutes. Cooking time: 10 minutes.
Total time: 25 minutes (plus 4 hours to chill).

. . . .

Per serving: Calories: 246   Fat: 21.9g   Saturated Fat: 13.4g   Protein: 1.8g
Carbohydrates: 9.6g   Fiber: 2.2g

12

Kitchen Staples

Homemade Mayonnaise

This is the way mayonnaise should taste: creamy, tangy, and oh so satisfying. Whether you use it as a sandwich spread or as a base for a salad dressing, this is the must-have mayonnaise to keep in your refrigerator.

Ingredient Tip: This recipe calls for a raw egg yolk. If you are concerned about consuming a raw egg, opt for pasteurized eggs at the grocery store.

1 egg yolk

1 tablespoon white wine vinegar

1 teaspoon Dijon mustard

1 cup extra-virgin olive oil

½ teaspoon salt

1. Combine the egg yolk, vinegar, and mustard in a food processor or blender. With the motor running, very slowly add the oil through the hole in the lid in a steady stream.
2. Put the mayonnaise in an airtight jar, stir in the salt, and cover. Refrigerate for up to 1 week.

Makes 1 cup. Prep time: 5 minutes.

Per serving (1 tablespoon):   Calories: 112   Fat: 12.9g   Saturated Fat: 1.9g
Protein: 0.2g   Carbohydrates: 0.1g   Fiber: 0g

Honey-Mustard Dipping Sauce

Vegetarian
Gluten-Free
Dairy-Free

This is sure to become your favorite sauce. The mayonnaise adds a creaminess to the sauce and creates a perfect balance with the tangy mustard and sweet honey. For a smoother texture, you may substitute plain Dijon mustard instead of the grainy mustard.

Serving Tip: Use this sauce to baste chicken or pork on the grill.

½ cup grainy Dijon mustard

½ cup honey

2 tablespoons Homemade Mayonnaise (page 288)

¼ teaspoon smoked paprika

In a small bowl, add the mustard, honey, mayonnaise, and smoked paprika and whisk well to combine. Store the sauce in an airtight lidded jar in the refrigerator for up to 1 week.

Makes about 1 cup. Prep time: 5 minutes.

Per serving (2 tablespoons): Calories: 94   Fat: 1.2g   Saturated Fat: 0g
Protein: 0.1g   Carbohydrates: 18.4g   Fiber: 0g

Spicy Chipotle Ketchup

Move over store-bought ketchup. This variety has no high-fructose corn syrup and is just what your French fries have been craving. The addition of the chipotle pepper lends spiciness and smokiness. You can find canned chipotle peppers in adobo sauce in the international aisle of the grocery. Omit the chipotle pepper if you'd like a more traditional-tasting ketchup.

Ingredient Tip: You can store the unused chipotle peppers in adobo sauce in an airtight jar in the refrigerator for up to 2 weeks. Stir chopped chipotle peppers into salsa, rice, or guacamole for a smoky kick.

1 (12-ounce) can tomato paste
1 chipotle pepper in adobo
    sauce, finely chopped
¼ cup honey
3 tablespoons water

2 tablespoons apple
    cider vinegar
1 teaspoon garlic powder
¼ teaspoon salt

Whisk together the tomato paste, chipotle pepper, honey, water, vinegar, garlic powder, and salt. Mix well to combine. Store the ketchup in an airtight container in the refrigerator for up to 2 weeks.

Makes about 1 cup. Prep time: 5 minutes.

. . . .

Per serving (1 tablespoon):   Calories: 36   Fat: 0.1g   Saturated Fat: 0g
Protein: 1g   Carbohydrates: 8.8g   Fiber: 0.9g

Smoky-Sweet Barbecue Sauce

Vegan
Gluten-Free

Barbecue sauce can be one of those polarizing ingredients, especially if you come from the barbecue belt in the South. This one is on the sweet side, so if you like a tangier, vinegar-based sauce, reduce the maple syrup or add some mustard.

Serving Tip: Whether on pork, chicken, or for dipping sweet potato fries, this sauce is great to have on hand. For especially busy nights, you can throw some chicken legs or pork chops on the grill and baste them with this sauce for a quick two-ingredient main dish.

½ cup tomato paste

½ cup water

¼ cup balsamic vinegar

¼ cup pure maple syrup

1 tablespoon tamari

2 garlic cloves, minced

1 teaspoon smoked paprika

½ teaspoon salt

½ teaspoon freshly ground black pepper

1 tablespoon avocado oil

1. In a medium saucepan, whisk together the tomato paste, water, vinegar, maple syrup, tamari, garlic, paprika, salt, and pepper.
2. Bring the mixture to a boil. Reduce the heat to medium and simmer for 5 minutes or until the sauce is thickened.
3. Remove the saucepan from the heat and stir in the avocado oil. Cool. Store in an airtight container in the refrigerator up to 1 week.

Makes about 1¼ cups. Prep time: 5 minutes. Cook time: 5 minutes. Total time: 10 minutes.

. . . .

Per serving (2 tablespoons): Calories: 37 Fat: 0.3g Saturated Fat: 0g
Protein: 0.9g Carbohydrates: 8.4g Fiber: 0.7g

Basil Pesto

Pesto is a classic Italian sauce and is handy to keep in the refrigerator for uses as a spread on sandwiches or a quick pasta sauce. In addition to basil, you can add other fresh herbs. Arugula or cilantro are great options for contributing different flavors.

Cooking Tip: To quickly and easily toast pine nuts, place them in a small skillet over medium heat. Swirl the pan occasionally and cook for 5 minutes or until the pine nuts are toasted. Due to their high fat content, they have a tendency to burn; watch them carefully while they cook.

2 cups firmly packed fresh
   basil leaves
3 garlic cloves
¼ cup pine nuts, toasted
½ cup extra-virgin olive oil

½ teaspoon salt
½ teaspoon freshly
   ground pepper
½ cup freshly grated
   Parmesan cheese

In a food processor, combine the basil, garlic, and pine nuts. Process until chopped. With the processor running, slowly add the oil in a steady stream. Process until smooth. Stir in the salt, pepper, and cheese.

Makes ¾ cup. Prep time: 10 minutes.

....

Per serving (1 tablespoon):   Calories: 108   Fat: 11.4g   Saturated Fat: 2g
Protein: 2.1g   Carbohydrates: 1g   Fiber: 0g

Homemade Marinara Sauce

This zippy sauce is a necessary staple. Whether you're making pizzas or pasta, it adds the perfect amount of flavor to every dish. Once you try it, you'll never want to buy jarred pasta sauce again. Even better, it's so easy to make.

Ingredient Tip: This recipe calls for chopped whole tomatoes in puree. Instead of draining them and saving the juice, use kitchen shears to snip the tomatoes right in the can. You'll have less mess and it'll save a ton of time.

2 tablespoons avocado oil

2 garlic cloves, sliced

¼ teaspoon crushed red pepper

2 (28-ounce) cans peeled whole tomatoes in puree, chopped

¼ cup chopped fresh basil

½ teaspoon salt

½ teaspoon freshly ground black pepper

1. In a medium saucepan over medium-high heat, heat the oil. Add the garlic and crushed red pepper. Cook for 2 minutes.
2. Add the tomatoes, basil, salt and pepper. Bring to a boil, reduce the heat to medium, and simmer, uncovered, for 30 minutes or until thickened.
3. Store the sauce in the refrigerator for up to 1 week or freeze for up to 2 months.

Makes 3 cups. Prep time: 5 minutes. Cooking time: 35 minutes. Total time: 40 minutes.

....

Per serving (¼ cup): Calories: 33 Fat: 0.3g Saturated Fat: 0g Protein: 1.3g Carbohydrates: 6.2g Fiber: 1.3g

Tzatziki Sauce

This quick-to-make and flavor-packed Greek condiment is a wonderful topping to grilled salmon, Falafel Pitas (page 185), or as a dip with Herbed Pita Chips (page 132). You can make it ahead, but as the days pass, the cucumber may cause it to become watery. It's still just as delicious to eat. To thicken it up again, just stir in additional Greek yogurt.

Ingredient Tip: Peeling and seeding the cucumber helps create the perfect texture of this sauce. You may omit this step if you'd like, or use a seedless English cucumber.

1 cup plain Greek yogurt

½ cup finely chopped peeled and seeded cucumber

¼ cup crumbled feta cheese

3 tablespoons lemon juice

1 tablespoon chopped fresh cilantro

1 teaspoon lemon zest

In a medium bowl, stir together the yogurt, cucumber, cheese, lemon juice, cilantro, and lemon zest. Store the sauce in an airtight container in the refrigerator for up to 2 days.

Makes about 1½ cups. Prep time: 10 minutes.

. . . .

Per serving (2 tablespoons):   Calories: 28   Fat: 1.5g   Saturated Fat: 1g
Protein: 2.1g   Carbohydrates: 1.6g   Fiber: 0g

Quick Olive-Pepper Tapenade

Tapenade is a delicious, traditional savory European spread for bread and crackers. Olives are a great low-calorie food full of heart-healthy monounsaturated fats that are believed to help lower bad cholesterol. They are also high in vitamin E, a natural antioxidant that protects against free radicals.

Serving Tip: Keep this briny dip on hand to spread on sandwiches, stir into a salad dressing, or to make a simple pasta sauce. It's also great mixed with a little Greek yogurt as a creamy olive dip.

1 roasted jarred red pepper

2 cups pitted Kalamata olives

¼ cup capers, drained

2 garlic cloves

1 tablespoon fresh oregano

1 tablespoon lemon juice

1 teaspoon lemon zest

½ cup extra-virgin olive oil

1. In a food processor, combine the pepper, olives, capers, garlic, oregano, lemon juice, and lemon zest. Pulse until combined.
2. With the food processor running, slowly add the oil in a steady stream. Store the tapenade in an airtight container in the refrigerator.

Makes 2 cups. Prep time: 5 minutes.

. . . .

Per serving (¼ cup):   Calories: 153   Fat: 16.3g   Saturated Fat: 2.3g
Protein: 0.6g   Carbohydrates: 3.6g   Fiber: 1.7g

Fresh Salsa

Making your own fresh salsa is easy, and you'll love the results. Depending on how hot you like your salsa, you can amp up the heat by not seeding the jalapeño. Or, increase the amount of jalapeño to two peppers. Either way, this fresh salsa is great to have around for a quick topping for dinner's meat or as a healthy snack with 100% whole-wheat tortilla chips.

Warning: When cutting jalapeños, you'll want to wear gloves or be sure to wash your hands well with soap and water. The oils can really burn if they get into your eyes or on your face.

3 tomatoes, finely chopped
½ cup finely chopped red onion
1 jalapeño pepper, seeded
    and minced
2 tablespoons fresh lime juice
2 tablespoons extra-virgin
    olive oil

¼ cup chopped fresh cilantro
1 teaspoon salt
1 teaspoon freshly ground
    black pepper
½ teaspoon ground cumin

In a large bowl, combine the tomatoes, onion, jalapeño, lime juice, oil, cilantro, salt, pepper, and cumin. Store the salsa in an airtight container for up to 2 weeks.

Makes 2 cups. Prep time: 10 minutes.

Per serving (¼ cup): Calories: 46   Fat: 3.6g   Saturated Fat: 0.5g
Protein: 0.6g   Carbohydrates: 3.7g   Fiber: 0.9g

Creamy Ranch-Style Dressing

This fresh take on everyone's favorite salad dressing will leave you feeling guilt-free. It's perfect served as a dip with fresh-cut vegetables, or as a traditional salad dressing. You can add a little water or broth to thin it out if you'd like.

Ingredient Tip: While the fresh herbs really make this dressing shine, if you don't have an herb garden or have them lying in your fridge, you can substitute dried herbs for fresh. Use about one-third the amount of dried for fresh.

1 cup plain Greek yogurt

½ cup sour cream

1 tablespoon lemon juice

2 garlic cloves, minced

2 tablespoons chopped
    fresh parsley

1 tablespoon chopped
    fresh chives

1 tablespoon chopped
    fresh dill

1 teaspoon smoked paprika

¼ teaspoon salt

¼ teaspoon freshly ground
    black pepper

In a medium bowl, stir together the yogurt, sour cream, lemon juice, garlic, parsley, chives, dill, smoked paprika, salt, and pepper. Store the dressing in an airtight container in the refrigerator for up to 3 days.

Makes 1 ½ cups. Prep time: 5 minutes.

....

Per serving (2 tablespoons): Calories: 41 Fat: 2.9g Saturated Fat: 1.8g
Protein: 2g Carbohydrates: 1.8g Fiber: 0g

Chunky Guacamole

Whether served with Baked Tortilla Chips (page 133), dolloped on tacos, or spread on toast, this simple dip will make you the hero at the next party. It comes together quickly and is full of fresh flavor.

Ingredient Tip: Use the lime juice to sprinkle over the avocado after they are cut so they don't turn brown.

2 avocados, chopped

1 tomato, chopped

1 jalapeño pepper, minced

2 garlic cloves, minced

3 tablespoons lime juice

¼ cup chopped fresh cilantro

½ teaspoon salt

½ teaspoon freshly ground
   black pepper

In a medium bowl, combine the avocados, tomato, jalapeño, garlic, lime juice, cilantro, salt, and pepper. Mash the guacamole with a fork to the desired consistency.

Makes 2 cups. Prep time: 5 minutes.

. . . .

Per serving (¼ cup):   Calories: 109   Fat: 9.8g   Saturated Fat: 2.1g
Protein: 1.2g   Carbohydrates: 5.9g   Fiber: 3.8g

Honey-Balsamic Vinaigrette

Vegan
Gluten-Free

This classic combination of honey, mustard, vinegar, and olive oil flavors is what makes a vinaigrette so great. It's a versatile condiment to serve on salads or to use as a marinade for chicken and pork.

Ingredient Variations: There are so many great flavored oils and vinegars. Try using them here. You may find fig-infused balsamic vinegar or blood orange–infused extra-virgin olive oil. It's fun and easy to create new dressings using this simple formula.

¼ cup balsamic vinegar

1 tablespoon honey

1 teaspoon Dijon mustard

¼ teaspoon salt

¼ teaspoon freshly ground black pepper

⅓ cup extra-virgin olive oil

In a small bowl, whisk together the vinegar, honey, mustard, salt, and pepper. Slowly add the oil in a steady stream, whisking until combined. Store the vinaigrette in an airtight container in the refrigerator for up to 2 weeks.

Makes about ⅔ cup. Prep time: 5 minutes.

. . . .

Per serving (1 tablespoon): Calories: 66 Fat: 6.7g Saturated Fat: 1g
Protein: 0g Carbohydrates: 1.9g Fiber: 0g

Cilantro-Lime Vinaigrette

This dressing is particularly harmonious with Mexican and Latin dishes. Serve it on taco salads or use it to flavor fresh salsas and guacamoles.

Storage Tip: Fresh cilantro is a handy, tasty herb to keep in the refrigerator. To help keep it fresh longer, remove the twist tie from the bunch and snip off the ends under cold running water. Wrap the bottom of the stalks in a damp paper towel and place the whole bunch in a large zip-top plastic bag. You'll have fresh cilantro for at least a week.

½ cup fresh lime juice

1 teaspoon grated lime zest

1 garlic clove, minced

3 tablespoons extra-virgin
    olive oil

1 tablespoon honey

½ teaspoon salt

½ teaspoon freshly ground
    black pepper

2 tablespoons chopped
    fresh cilantro

In a small bowl, whisk together the lime juice, lime zest, garlic, oil, honey, salt, pepper, and cilantro. Store the vinaigrette in an airtight container in the refrigerator for up to 3 days.

Makes about ¾ cup. Prep time: 5 minutes.

. . . .

Per serving (2 tablespoons):   Calories: 74   Fat: 7g   Saturated Fat: 1g
Protein: 0.1g   Carbohydrates: 3.8g   Fiber: 0g

Mustard-Thyme Vinaigrette

Vegan
Gluten-Free

After one taste of this simple vinaigrette, you'll make dressings from scratch every time. This one uses dried thyme, but adding fresh thyme makes it even more delicious. Experiment with other diced fresh herbs like tarragon and rosemary.

Ingredient Tip: To quickly peel garlic, place the clove on a cutting board. Cover it with the flat side of a chef's knife. In a swift motion, hit the knife with the heel of your hand. The papery peel with come off quickly.

1 garlic clove, minced

⅓ cup white wine vinegar

1 tablespoon honey

1 tablespoon Dijon mustard

½ teaspoon dried thyme

½ teaspoon salt

½ teaspoon freshly ground black pepper

In a small bowl, whisk together the garlic, vinegar, honey, mustard, thyme, salt, and pepper. Store the vinaigrette in an airtight container in the refrigerator for up to 2 weeks.

Makes ½ cup. Prep time: 5 minutes.

. . . .

Per serving (1 tablespoon): Calories: 12 Fat: 0.1g Saturated Fat: 0g Protein: 0.1g Carbohydrates: 2.6g Fiber: 0g

Creamy Caesar Dressing

This creamy dressing is the perfect accompaniment for crunchy romaine lettuce leaves, freshly grated Parmesan-Reggiano cheese, and 100% whole-wheat croutons. It also makes a good basting sauce for chicken and pork.

Ingredient Tip: Like classic Caesar dressing, this recipe calls for anchovies, which may not appeal to some. The anchovies serve to add a briny flavor to the dressing, but feel free to omit them if you'd like.

½ cup plain Greek yogurt

2 tablespoons lemon juice

1 tablespoon white
    wine vinegar

1 tablespoon Dijon mustard

2 garlic cloves

2 teaspoons anchovy paste

¼ teaspoon salt

¼ teaspoon freshly ground
    black pepper

¼ cup extra-virgin olive oil

1. In a food processor, combine the yogurt, lemon juice, vinegar, mustard, garlic, anchovy paste, salt, and pepper. Process until smooth.

2. With the food processor running, add the oil in a slow, steady stream. Store the dressing in an airtight glass container in the refrigerator for up to 1 week.

Makes about 1 cup. Prep time: 10 minutes.

. . . .

Per serving (1 tablespoon):   Calories: 37   Fat: 4.4g   Saturated Fat: 0.7g
Protein: 0.8g   Carbohydrates: 0.6g   Fiber: 0g

Asian Marinade

Vegan
Gluten-Free

Unlike store-bought teriyaki marinades, this one has no sign of high-fructose corn syrup anywhere. It is the perfect marinade for all types of meats and even tofu. Or, use it as a dipping sauce.

Ingredient Tip: The next time you buy a fresh, cored pineapple, save the juice from the bottom of the container. It's guaranteed not to have any additional sweeteners in it.

½ cup unsweetened pineapple juice

½ cup organic reduced-sodium vegetable broth

3 tablespoons tamari or coconut aminos

3 tablespoons brown rice vinegar

2 tablespoons honey

1 tablespoon dark sesame oil

1 tablespoon grated fresh ginger

2 garlic cloves, minced

In a medium bowl, whisk together the pineapple juice, broth, tamari, vinegar, honey, oil, ginger, and garlic. Store the marinade in an airtight container in the refrigerator for up to 1 week.

Makes about 1 ½ cups. Prep time: 10 minutes.

Per serving (2 tablespoons):   Calories: 35   Fat: 1.2g   Saturated Fat: 0g
Protein: 0.8g   Carbohydrates: 5g   Fiber: 0g

Creamy Natural Peanut Butter

After you make this homemade peanut butter and realize how easy it is, you may not buy prepared peanut butter again. The trick to making peanut butter is having a little patience. As the peanuts puree, they will naturally release their oils to create a creamy product.

Ingredient Variations: Try making other nut butters like cashew butter and almond butter.

4 cups dry-roasted peanuts   **1 tablespoon honey**

1. In a food processor, combine the peanuts and honey. Process for 2 to 3 minutes, stopping to scrape down the sides occasionally.
2. Store the peanut butter in an airtight container in the refrigerator for up to 1 month.

Makes about 2 cups. Prep time: 10 minutes.

....

Per serving (1 tablespoon):   Calories: 82   Fat: 7g   Saturated Fat: 1g
Protein: 3.5g   Carbohydrates: 3.5g   Fiber: 1g

Warm Berry Sauce

This warm compote is the perfect balance between sweet and tart and is great for adding to plain Greek yogurt, topping Yogurt Cheesecake Bars (page 274), or just eating by the spoonful.

Ingredient Tip: Do you ever start juicing lemons only to realize there's hardly any juice in them? To get the most juice out of a lemon, pick those that seem heavy for their size and are easy to press when squeezed. Before slicing into them, give them a quick roll with your palm to mash the pulp and get the juice flowing.

¼ cup lemon juice

¼ cup water

2 teaspoons arrowroot powder

3 tablespoons honey

2 cups frozen mixed berries

¼ teaspoon lemon zest

In a small saucepan, combine lemon juice, water, arrowroot powder, and honey. Stir in the berries and lemon zest. Bring to a boil. Reduce the heat to medium and simmer for 5 minutes, or until the berries begin to lose shape. Remove the saucepan from heat and let cool until warm. Or, cool completely, cover, and refrigerate for up to 1 week.

Makes about 1 cup. Prep time: 5 minutes. Cooking time: 5 minutes. Total time: 10 minutes.

Per serving (2 tablespoons):   Calories: 49   Fat: 0.2g   Saturated Fat: 0g
Protein: 0.3g   Carbohydrates: 11.6g   Fiber: 1.3g

Chocolate Sauce

This fudgy sauce is great to have around for a quick dessert option. Pour it over fresh strawberries or homemade ice cream, or stir it into Greek yogurt for a quick treat.

Serving Tip: If making this sauce ahead or enjoying leftovers, the sauce will need to be melted to serve. You can either zap it in the microwave for 10 seconds or reheat it gently in a small saucepan.

16 ounces 70% bittersweet chocolate, chopped

1 cup coconut milk

2 tablespoons honey

1 teaspoon pure vanilla extract

1. In a medium saucepan, combine the chocolate, coconut milk, and honey. Cook over medium-low heat for 10 to 15 minutes, stirring constantly until the mixture is smooth. Stir in the vanilla.
2. Store the sauce in an airtight glass container in the refrigerator for up to 2 weeks.

Makes 2 cups. Prep time: 5 minutes. Cooking time: 10 minutes. Total time: 15 minutes.

. . . .

Per serving (2 tablespoons):   Calories: 195   Fat: 12g   Saturated Fat: 9.1g
Protein: 2.5g   Carbohydrates: 19.9g   Fiber: 1.3g

Coconut Whipped Cream

This is a magical trick to making clean eating–friendly whipped cream. The liquid you reserve can be used in smoothies in place of almond or cow's milk. Add a dash of nutmeg, ground cinnamon, or cardamom for a subtly spiced whipped cream.

Ingredient Tip: To easily pour off the coconut liquid, try opening the can from the bottom. The solids will stay at the top and make it easier to spoon out.

1 (15-ounce) can coconut milk, chilled overnight
2 tablespoons honey

1 tablespoon pure vanilla extract

1. Carefully open the can of coconut milk. Spoon out the thick cream on top into a medium bowl. Reserve the coconut liquid for another use.
2. Add the honey and vanilla extract. Beat the mixture with a hand-held mixer until fluffy. Keep the cream refrigerated in an airtight container for up to 3 days until ready to serve.

Makes 1 cup. Prep time: 10 minutes.

. . . .

Per serving (1 tablespoon): Calories: 71 Fat: 6.3g Saturated Fat: 5.6g
Protein: 0.6g Carbohydrates: 3.7g Fiber: 0.6g

Appendix A
28 Days of Clean Eating at a Glance

This chart lists every breakfast, lunch, and dinner selected for your month of clean eating. Visit each week's section in chapter 3 for additional information on daily snack recommendations and dessert.

	WEEK ONE	WEEK TWO
Day One	**B:** Streusel-Topped Blueberry Muffins **L:** Mediterranean Turkey Wrap **D:** Salmon with Citrus Salsa and Steamed Green Beans	**B:** Hash Brown Scramble **L:** Southwestern Salad with Shrimp and Black Beans **D:** Slow-Cooked Italian Pot Roast and Vegetables
Day Two	**B:** Triple-Berry Smoothie **L:** Almond Butter–Apple Sandwiches **D:** Braised Pork Loin with Dried Figs and Roasted Asparagus	**B:** Almond, Cherry, and Vanilla Smoothie **L:** Corn and Potato Chowder **D:** Mushroom Barley Risotto
Day Three	**B:** Pumpkin-Pecan Breakfast Cookies **L:** Three-Bean Farro Salad **D:** Curried Chickpeas with Spinach and Brown Rice	**B:** Nutty Whole-Grain Waffles **L:** Pasta Salad with Avocado-Pesto Cream Sauce **D:** Lemon-Garlic Roasted Chicken with Steamed Broccoli and Wild Rice
Day Four	**B:** Spinach–Red Pepper Frittata with Feta **L:** Turkey-Cucumber Sandwich with Mashed Avocado **D:** Peanut Noodles with Shredded Pork and Vegetables	**B:** Slow Cooker Overnight Oatmeal with Fresh Cherries and Maple Syrup **L:** Chicken-Pesto BLT **D:** Shredded Beef Tacos
Day Five	**B:** Tropical Smoothie **L:** Creamy Asparagus Soup **D:** Grilled Honey-Mustard Chicken with Marinated Tomatoes and Cucumbers	**B:** Avocado-Lime Smoothie **L:** Tuna-Barley Salad with Roasted Red Peppers and Artichokes **D:** Grilled Portobello Burgers with Sweet Potato Fries
Day Six	**B:** Eggs Baked in Toast Cups **L:** Chicken-Quinoa Salad with Oranges, Olives, and Feta **D:** Grilled Mini Veggie Pizzas	**B:** Streusel-Topped Blueberry Muffins **L:** Minestrone Soup **D:** Thai Shrimp and Snow Pea Curry
Day Seven	**B:** Scrambled Egg, Black Bean, and Avocado Breakfast Burritos **L:** Curried Vegetable Soup **D:** Chicken Breasts Stuffed with Roasted Red Peppers, Olives, and Feta	**B:** Mango Lassi Smoothie **L:** Beef and Goat Cheese Quesadillas **D:** Chicken Pasta Puttanesca

	WEEK THREE	WEEK FOUR
Day One	**B:** Eggs Poached in Spiced Tomato Sauce **L:** Black Bean Soup **D:** Shepherd's Pie	**B:** Banana Nut Bread **L:** Corn and Potato Chowder **D:** Loaded Pinto Bean Nachos
Day Two	**B:** Banana, Strawberry, and Walnut Smoothie **L:** Mediterranean Turkey Wrap **D:** Sausage, Lentil, and Kale Stew	**B:** Peach-Oat Smoothie **L:** Black Bean Soup **D:** Skillet-Barbecued Chicken with Mustard Green Bean–Potato Salad
Day Three	**B:** Mini Spinach, Pepper, and Cheese Quiches **L:** Minestrone Soup **D:** Flounder Piccata with Sun-Dried Tomato Rice Pilaf	**B:** Vegetable Omelet with Goat Cheese **L:** Almond Butter–Apple Sandwiches **D:** Grilled Flank Steak with Cucumber, Tomato, and Corn Relish
Day Four	**B:** Baked Banana French Toast **L:** Three-Bean Farro Salad **D:** Mini Meatloaves with Mashed Potatoes and Green Beans	**B:** Green Tea, Cucumber, and Mint Smoothie and Toast with Creamy Natural Peanut Butter **L:** Southwestern Salad with Shrimp and Black Beans **D:** Pork and Peach Skewers with Grilled Asparagus
Day Five	**B:** Ginger-Coconut Smoothie **L:** Pasta Salad with Avocado-Pesto Cream Sauce **D:** Panko-Pecan Crusted Chicken Tenders with Steamed Broccoli	**B:** Yogurt-Berry Parfait **L:** Chicken-Pesto BLT **D:** Sweet Chili-Tofu and Sugar Snap Stir-Fry
Day Six	**B:** South-of-the-Border Breakfast Strata **L:** Turkey-Cucumber Sandwiches with Mashed Avocado **D:** Falafel Pitas with Tzatziki Sauce	**B:** Pumpkin-Pecan Breakfast Cookies **L:** Black Bean Soup **D:** Maple-Sage Pork Tenderloin with Sautéed Mushroom Farro
Day Seven	**B:** Banana Nut Bread **L:** Tuna-Barley Salad with Roasted Red Peppers and Artichokes **D:** Beet, Pear, and Mixed Greens Salad	**B:** Chocolate–Peanut Butter Smoothie **L:** Creamy Asparagus Soup **D:** Coconut Shrimp with Sesame Green Beans

Appendix B
Seasonal Eating
Fruits and Vegetables

Enjoying fruits and vegetables at their peak is easy with this handy guide to seasonal produce. If you have a craving for something that's out of season, check the frozen foods aisle; you might find it there.

Spring

Artichokes	Cauliflower	Rhubarb
Arugula	Fennel	Spinach
Asparagus	Green beans	Strawberries
Broccoli	Peas	Sugar snap peas
Bibb lettuce	Radicchio	
Chard	Radishes	

Summer

Apricots	Grapes	Summer squash
Bell peppers	Green beans	Tomatoes
Blackberries	Honeydew	Turnips
Blueberries	Hot peppers	Watermelon
Broccoli	Kale	Zucchini
Cantaloupe	Nectarines	
Celery	Okra	
Cherries	Peaches	
Corn	Plums	
Cucumbers	Radishes	
Eggplant	Raspberries	
Endive	Snow peas	
Figs	Sugar snap peas	

Fall

Acorn squash

Broccoli

Broccoli rabe

Brussels sprouts

Butternut squash

Cauliflower

Cranberries

Fennel

Grapes

Kale

Pears

Pomegranates

Pumpkins

Winter

Acorn squash

Brussels sprouts

Butternut squash

Clementines

Collard greens

Grapefruit

Kale

Kiwi

Oranges

Pears

Pomegranate

Potatoes

Sweet potatoes

Tangerines

Appendix C
The Dirty Dozen and the Clean Fifteen

Eating Clean

Each year, the Environmental Working Group, an environmental organization based in the United States, publishes a list they call the "Dirty Dozen." These are the fruits and vegetables that, when conventionally grown using chemical pesticides and fertilizers, carry the highest residues. If organically grown isn't an option for you, simply avoid these fruits and vegetables altogether. The list is updated each year, but here is the most recent list (2014).

Similarly, the Environmental Working Group publishes a list of "The Clean 15," fruits and vegetables that, even when conventionally grown, contain very low levels of chemical pesticide or fertilizer residue. These items are acceptable to purchase conventionally grown.

You might want to snap a photo of these two lists and keep them on your phone to reference while shopping. Or you can download the Environmental Working Group's app to your phone or tablet.

THE DIRTY DOZEN

APPLE
BELL PEPPER
CELERY
CHERRY TOMATO
CUCUMBER
GRAPE
NECTARINE,
   IMPORTED
PEACH
POTATO
SNAP PEA
SPINACH
STRAWBERRY

THE CLEAN FIFTEEN

ASPARAGUS
AVOCADO
CABBAGE
CANTALOUPE
CORN
EGGPLANT
GRAPEFRUIT
KIWI
MANGO
MUSHROOM
ONION
PAPAYA
PINEAPPLE
SWEET PEAS
   (FROZEN)
SWEET POTATO

Conversion Charts

Volume Equivalents (Liquid)

U.S. STANDARD (OUNCES)	U.S. STANDARD (APPROXIMATE)	METRIC
2 tablespoons	1 fl. ounce	30 milliliters
¼ cup	2 fl. ounces	60 milliliters
½ cup	4 fl. ounces	120 milliliters
1 cup	8 fl. ounces	240 milliliters
1½ cups	12 fl. ounces	355 milliliters
2 cups or 1 pint	16 fl. ounces	475 milliliters
4 cups or 1 quart	32 fl. ounces	1 liter
1 gallon	128 fl. ounces	4 liters

Oven Temperatures

FAHRENHEIT (F)	CELSIUS (C) (APPROXIMATE)
250	120
300	150
325	165
350	180
375	190
400	200
425	220
450	230

Volume Equivalents (Dry)

U.S. STANDARD	METRIC (APPROXIMATE)
⅛ teaspoon	0.5 milliliters
¼ teaspoon	1 milliliter
½ teaspoon	2 milliliters
¾ teaspoon	4 milliliters
1 teaspoon	5 milliliters
1 tablespoon	15 milliliters
¼ cup	59 milliliters
⅓ cup	79 milliliters
½ cup	118 milliliters
⅔ cup	156 milliliters
¾ cup	177 milliliters
1 cup	235 milliliters
2 cups or 1 pint	475 milliliters
3 cups	700 milliliters
4 cups or 1 quart	1 liter
½ gallon	2 liters
1 gallon	4 liters

Weight Equivalents

U.S. STANDARD	METRIC (APPROXIMATE)
½ ounce	15 grams
1 ounce	30 grams
2 ounces	60 grams
4 ounces	115 grams
8 ounces	225 grams
12 ounces	340 grams
16 ounces or 1 pound	455 grams

References

Academy of Nutrition and Dietetics. "Surprise! This Is Processed Too!" Accessed June 5, 2014. www.eatright.org/Public/content .aspx?id=6442471055.

Alzheimer's Association. "Adopt a Brain-Healthy Diet." Alz.org. Accessed July 10, 2014. www.alz.org/we_can_help_adopt_a_brain _healthy_diet.asp.

Banas, Timothy. "Which Plastic Containers Can I Safely Use?" Livestrong.com. Accessed July 9, 2014. www.livestrong.com /article/158674-which-plastic-containers-can-i-safely-use/.

Celiac Disease Foundation. "What is Gluten?" Accessed June 12, 2014. http://celiac.org/live-gluten-free/gluten-free-diet/what -is-gluten/.

Davis, Jeanie Lerche. "25 Top Heart-Healthy Foods." WebMD. Accessed June 4, 2014. www.webmd.com/food-recipes/features /25-top-heart-healthy-foods.

Environmental Working Group. "EWG's 2014 Shopper's Guide to Pesticides in Produce." Accessed July 10, 2014. www.ewg.org /foodnews/.

Gardner, Amanda. "14 Best and Worst Foods for Digestion." *Health.* Accessed June 4, 2014. www.health.com/health/gallery /0,,20551987,00.html.

Gómez-Pinilla, Fernando. "Brain Foods: The Effects of Nutrients on Brain Function." *Nature Reviews Neuroscience* 9 (July 2008), 568–78. doi:10.1038/nrn2421.

Hastings, Deborah. "The 25 Best Foods for Your Heart." Prevention. Accessed June 4, 2014. www.prevention.com/health /health-concerns/best-foods-heart-health.

Huffington Post. "Brain Food: Superfoods to Improve Your Cognitive Function." Last modified September 30, 2013. www.huffingtonpost.com/2012/09/18/brain-food-superfoods _n_1895328.html.

Lin, Lin, Hanja Allemekinders, Angela Dansby, Lisa Campbell, Shaunda Durace-Tod, Alvin Berger, and Peter J. H. Jones. "Evidence of Health Benefits of Canola Oil." *Nutrition Reviews* 71, no. 6 (June 2013): 370-85. doi:10.1111/nure.12033.

Main, Emily. "45 Good Reasons to Ditch Junk Food." Rodale News. February 21, 2012. www.rodalenews.com/phosphate-foods#.

Mercola, Joseph. "Coconut Oil Benefits: When Fat Is Good for You." Huffington Post. Last modifed May 25, 2011. www.huffingtonpost.com /dr-mercola/coconut-oil-benefits_b_821453.html.

Sorgen, Carol. "Eat Smart for a Healthier Brain." WebMD. Accessed June 3, 2014. www.webmd.com/diet/features/eat-smart -healthier-brain.

"The World's Healthiest Foods." Accessed June 20, 2014. www.whfoods.com/index.php.

Vann, Madeline. "Superfoods That Help Digestion." Everyday Health. Last modified September 4, 2013. www.everydayhealth.com /digestive-health-pictures/superfoods-that-help-digestion.aspx# /slide-1.

Whole Grains Council. "Identifying Whole Grain Products." Accessed June 12, 2014. http://wholegrainscouncil.org/whole -grains-101/identifying-whole-grain-products.

Wolpert, Stuart. "Scientists Learn How What You Eat Affects Your Brain—and Those of Your Kids." UCLA Newsroom. Accessed July 9, 2008. http://newsroom.ucla.edu/releases/scientists-learn-how -food-affects-52668.

Zeratsky, Katerine. "What Is BPA, and What Are the Concerns about BPA?" Mayo Clinic, Nutrition and Healthy Eating. Accessed May 21, 2013. www.mayoclinic.org/healthy-living/nutrition-and -healthy-eating/expert-answers/bpa/faq-20058331.

Recipe Index

Index